WA

Transformation Management by Harmony

WA

Transformation Management by Harmony

Yuji Kishira

Additional copies can be obtained from your local bookstore or the publisher:

The North River Press
Publishing Corporation
P.O. Box 567
Great Barrington, MA 01230

www.northriverpress.com

ISBN: 978-0-88427-191-8

Copyright © 2009 Yuji Kishira

All rights reserved. No part of this book may be reproduced in any form or by any electronic or mechanical means, including information storage and retrieval systems, without permission in writing from the publisher.

Printed in the United States of America

Acknowledgments

I am deeply grateful to Dr. Eliyahu M. Goldratt who kindly spent time offering me guidance on a one-on-one basis during his visit to Japan, appreciated my achievements and motivated me to write this book. I received much valuable advice and guidance on Critical Chain Project Management from my best friends at Afinitus Group, LLC: Mr. David Updegrove, Mr. Hilbert Robinson, Mr. Rodger Morrison and Ms. Elaine Frost, and from Satoru Murakami, president of Goal System Consulting Inc. I would like to take this opportunity to thank all of you.

I would also like to thank Tadashi Onishi, Chairman, Chubu Region Quality Control Association for providing valuable advice toward a guiding principle going forward, "from visualization of the sites to visualization of management for autonomic Kaizen."

My lovely wife, Mayuko, author of various picture books for children, is always my inspiration. When I was writing, she was illustrating the bugs according the text, which stimulate me evolving the text further. The author of picture book express many things with short sentence which amazes me always. If you find this book easy and friendly to understand, it is thanks to her valuable advice.

Contents

Introduction: Bugs in the Company

The most common complaints during a project are as follows:

- -Can't have a sufficient budget
- -Can't have sufficient resources
- -Can't get timely responses from customers
- -Can't share information among all project stakeholders in timely manner
- -Can't get deliveries on time from the suppliers
- -Can't have a stable scope of the project during the project
- -Can't get support from other people
- -Can't get management support

If these problems stay in the company long, it becomes a very serious situation where you begin to see "Can't do Bugs" and "Should Bugs" prevailing everywhere.

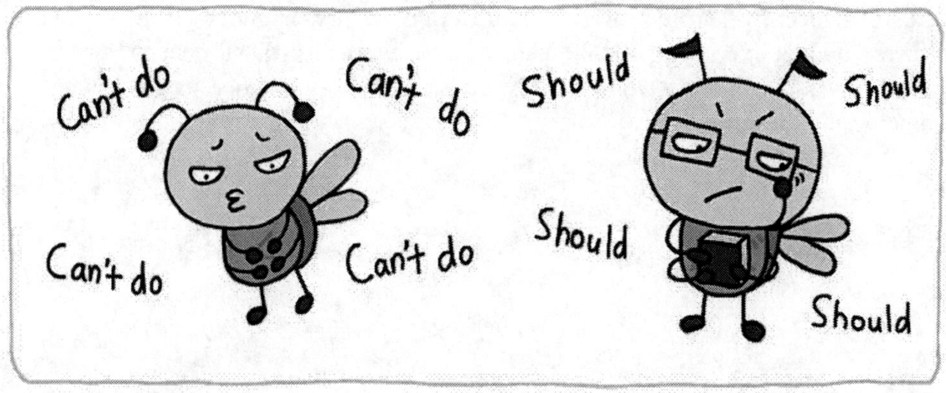

"Can't do Bugs" repeatedly sing, "Can't do, can't do, can't do..." in a helpless tone, while "Should Bugs" sing a little bit differently. They sing, "Should, should, should..." as in, "We should...You should...Our management should..." Both "Can't do Bugs" and "Should Bugs" look similar, as shown in the previous figure, but "Should Bugs" can be identified by their larger heads and eyeglasses. They are often observed carrying several management books in their hands, too. For some unknown reason they have a tendency to be addicted to three-character acronyms, like XYZ management methods.

Although they are categorized as different types of bugs, they are considered to have originated from a common ancestor because of the following characteristics:

-Move in the holes and corners
-Love damp places (conversation)
-Don't move out from the safe places
-Always searching the problems outside of themselves
-Strongly infectious

Years of extensive research have finally disclosed the main infection routes in the following two places:

-Smoking room
-Cheap Izakaya (Japanse tavern) near the company

Special caution is needed in regards to the cheap Izakaya neighboring the company. Some recent studies disclosed that the chance of infection is dramatically increased in cases of a cheap Izakaya with an estimated budget of less than 3000 Yen per person, where people tend to discuss company projects, often spreading "Can't do" and "Should" bugs through word of mouth. A breakthrough prescription was recently developed to combat against it. The solution is to go to a restaurant with an estimated budget exceeding 5000 Yen per person, where you will enjoy delicious food along with premier drinks, like fine wine. In such a place, you know that discussing company projects can spoil all the fun of the food, and you naturally choose much more interesting topics, like your hobbies. However, I recently learned an even more effective prescription: Go to a place with estimated budget exceeding 10,000 Yen, where beautiful girls sit next to you, and you naturally start to talk about your dreams, love, etc.... Sounds good to me. I want to try it sometime in the future.

Yuji Kishira

Part 1 KEIEI KAIKAKU – Managing Transformation Projects

Session 01 The Inseparable Relationship Between "Management" and "Projects"

Management reform projects, personnel system projects, mid-term management plan projects, cost reduction projects, productivity improvement projects, yield improvement projects, lead time reduction projects, supply chain management projects, six sigma projects, balanced score card projects, new product development projects, research and development projects, marketing projects, brand management projects, and public administration reform projects...

Management activities and project activities have an inseparable relationship. In reality, management itself can justifiably be said to be a continuous practice of leading multiple projects on a daily basis. Managing these projects to success is very much related to company performance; it may even be a life or death issue if the project is crucial to the company. However, the reality of managing projects to success is really difficult in many cases.

Each project is unique, never exactly the same as the previous one. In most cases, mass-produced goods are not thought to be associated with projects. However, reality belies this idea. There are continuous cycles of on-going projects in mass production. They start with research and development projects, proceed to product development projects, and then to mass production line start-up projects. Once a new product is launched, the yield improvement projects, six sigma projects, productivity enhancement projects, cost reduction projects, lead time reduction projects, supply chain management projects, etc., begin. Continuous improvement projects are a

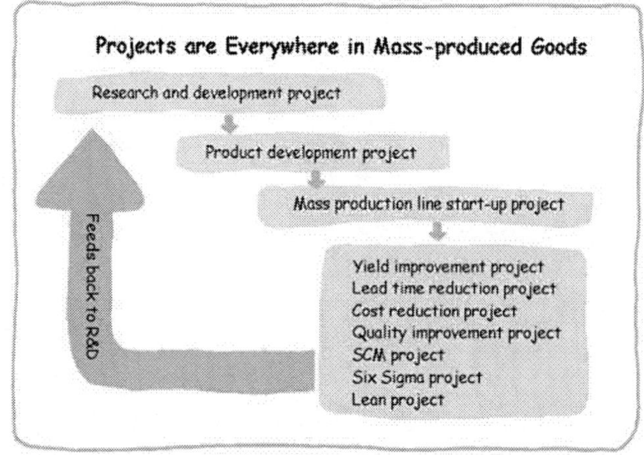

necessity for surviving severe competition in the marketplace. When we face big technical issues or other challenges, they are fed back to research and development, and the research and development projects start again. These repeated cycles are a reality in the life cycle of mass-produced goods.

In daily life we use the word "project" often. What is the meaning of this word "project"? According to the *Project & Program Management for Enterprise Innovation (P2M)* standard guidebook, a project is a "value creation undertaking for the future, with a specific mission in a specific period, with beginning and end subject to constraints such as resources, situations, etc."

For corporate management, undesirable effects in the organization are often the motivation to start projects. It is commonly said, "The problem is a gap between the ideality (to be) and the reality (as is)." This gap often triggers projects aimed to make the company better. Each year annual budgets are planned for the next fiscal year. Analyzing the current situation, considering the current business environment, and assuming the gap between ideality and reality, the budget and action plans are discussed and approved, and it becomes the company's formal fiscal year plan. These plans are often given to the project teams in the format of "Projects." It is not an exaggeration to say the accomplishment of these projects plays a key role in corporate management performance. In other words, managing projects to success is really *management itself.* Thus, project management is getting more and more attention than ever before. This is especially true for companies struggling to survive in the ever-changing, severely competitive market.

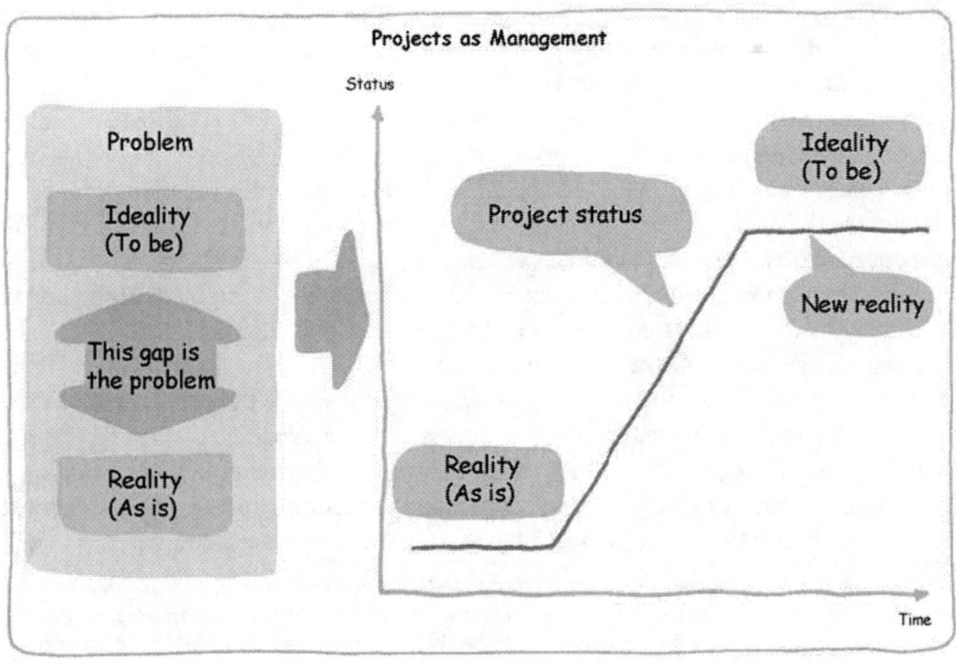

Session 02 Why do Projects Fail?

Projects are everywhere in our daily lives. When we plan or propose something new in the company, the first thing we generally discuss is the start-up of a new project. "Let's start a new project!" is voiced with full enthusiasm. However, often the enthusiasm gradually wanes as projects progress, and in many cases it seems extremely difficult to reach the goal after all. There are too many projects, during which the question is asked:

"What was the purpose of this project?"

Contrary to the opinions of some, project members aren't lazy; actually, it's quite the opposite, most work seriously and very hard. However, as they are executed, projects tend to gradually drift in a direction away from what was first conceived. The confusion becomes especially severe in the management reform projects, where so-called "three-character acronym management methods" are constantly being introduced one after another.[1] Employees and managers are continually subjected to learning new management methods; a newer technique will be introduced almost as soon as one method is studied and implemented in practice.[2] One often hears, "There are problems with the current method. This new method is the quintessential solution for all the problems blocking our success. Great case studies are coming from western countries." But when we revisit the projects, it becomes obvious that we have the exact same problems as before, and the project team faces growing resistance against the method that was just recently implemented. After a little research, we find that other companies using the same method aren't getting the results either, and it becomes apparent that a particular method hardly works well in Japanese business and now we must study a new method.

1. I am not saying that three-character management methods are always bad. TOC has three characters. However, I feel better that CCPM (Critical Chain Project Management) has four characters.

2. Some people refer to their presentations as "fireworks." It is beautiful in a flash but disappears fast. However, sometimes they are necessary in boring management meetings. So, "fireworks" presentations are infiltrating into management meetings everywhere.

But what about the current method? It was just implemented through painful effort on everyone's part; isn't it necessary to continue until some result is seen? Maybe, however the new method sounds more attractive…

There are many cases of projects failing in such a "twist and turn" atmosphere; often they end with a "positive" cancellation speech: "Everybody, thank you very much for your hard work. This project has achieved some[3] results, and will be positively cancelled." Sometimes, projects are vaguely dissolved (or evaporated away) and there isn't even a ceremony for a "positive cancellation." Regardless, from the beginning, most project members do not know the criteria of successful projects, so nobody knows whether their projects are a success or not.

Problems with Projects

In most cases, the problems in projects include the following:

- The goal is not clear across the project team.
- The "means" become the objectives of the project.
- Teamwork and support from other parties are not always obtained during projects.

Are these problems inherent to the chosen "method"? If we find project successes in some cases, there might not be a problem with the "method." What then, is the solution?

- "Let's have a clear, common goal!"
- "Don't confuse objectives with means!"
- "Teamwork is important!"

We very often hear these phrases broadcast throughout the project environment. In fact, these maxims are nothing new, and everyone understands them as common sense. Senior management continually insists: "Let's have a clear common goal!" "Don't confuse objectives with means!" and "Teamwork is important!" These are written in management books, in training texts and as management slogans posted on the wall. The project members also understand the importance, and always consider them. But, in spite of their best efforts, we still have the same problems. Why?

---

3. Honestly, I have never had a good understanding of word of "some" but I know I should not ask such a question to my boss.

Talking about Management or Talking about Mentality?

Management cannot leave such a situation unaddressed for long, and usually starts working on management reform. The following phrases begin to be proclaimed loudly across the organization: "profit improvement"; "customer satisfaction"; "growing organization"; "human resource development"; "successful projects"; "motivation"; "trust among organization members"; "shorten lead times"; "quality improvement"; "take action before it's too late"; "mind-set of management"; "teamwork"; "flexible organization"; "hands-on experience and know-how"; "cooperation across the organization"; "prioritize"; "focus"; "create flexibility"; "visibility"; "Kaizen"; "report ASAP"; "understanding by management"; "sense of urgency", and so on.

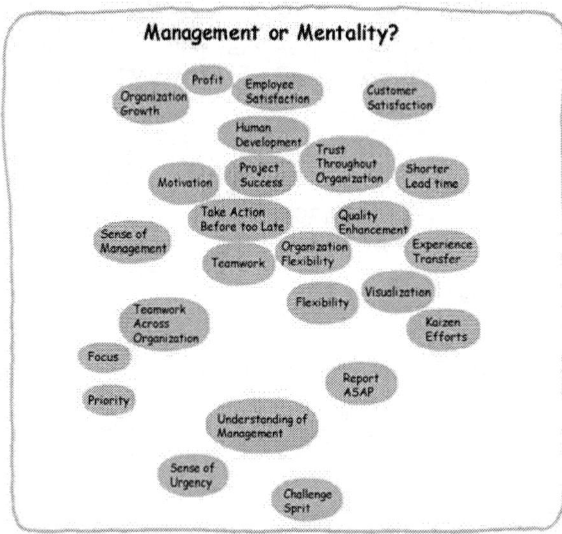

These are mostly good things for the organization, common sense ideas with which most of us can agree. However, if we try to apply them in the real world, things get very tough. This is because in the real world multiple departments (often with different priorities) and outside parties (which have their own objectives) are associated in complicated arrangements. In this situation, if we fall into philosophical discussions (people's mind-sets), though they are not necessarily bad in and of themselves, we sometimes take too long to resolve project issues, which are often critical and urgent.

Do Problems Exist Inside the Project or Outside the Project?

The reality of a project is very difficult. Budget, resources, and available time for a project are often inadequate, and the difficulty of the situation is increased by the severe competition of the marketplace. Decisions from the client or management can be slow, information may not be shared in a timely manner, and delivery from suppliers is sometimes delayed. Moreover, a project's scope changes and often "creeps." Even if there are serious problems, support is not necessarily obtained from management, or from other project stakeholders, in a timely manner. In spite of such circumstances, project members work very hard, with a strong sense of responsibility and urgency, and are willing to work even around the clock to comply with all kinds of expectations from stakeholders. So, looking carefully into these problems, it becomes quite obvious that they do not originate inside the project, they exist outside of the project.

I have an offer for you. What if you could obtain an adequate budget and resources (on time), have a good deal of safety time, get swift decisions by customers and management, have information shared in a timely manner, have far less supplier delivery delays, and have any changes managed with teamwork, getting support from other project teams and senior management across the organization? What would you think if I told you that you can obtain all of these things by just slightly changing the way you show the project status, and without changing most of your current daily project practices? Is this something worth trying?[4]

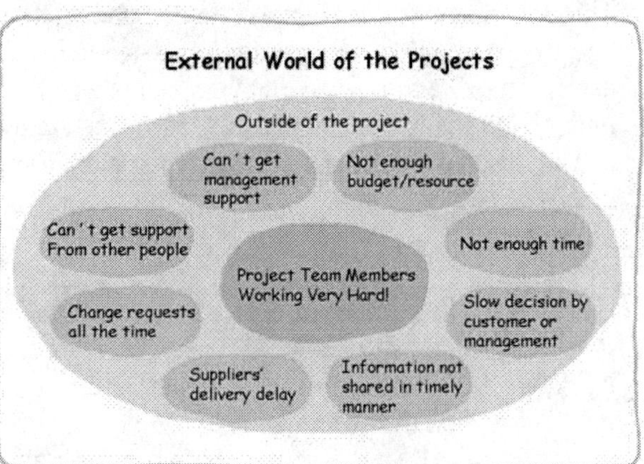

Be Careful of Methods Abuse

Many methods for management reform exist. It is impossible to escape the temptation to try some, since every method seems to have merit, along with some fascinating catchwords. When a new management method gets popular in a particular industry, it is tested in a pilot study to find out if it might be useful. After the effect is analyzed, and if it is found to be good, it is recommended for the next test projects. Here and there in the enterprise, test projects come to exist because management methods are actively being developed one after another.

The side effects are sometimes intense for project members when the new methods are continuously tested one after another.[1] In order to suppress the side effects, a newly developed, more powerful method needs to be tested. With a continuous dose of a variety of management methods, people become more and more intoxicated (obsessed) with the need for more new methods. Finally, they feel uneasy if they don't continuously adopt new methods. Now it is getting serious.

1. New methods are sometimes called "Best practices," as in, "Here, we have five best practices. Choose one for testing to see if it works." It sounds like new drug testing, doesn't it?

4. Whenever I make this statement in my presentations, almost everyone looks at me with distrust. In fact, I was once a skeptic myself. Even after all the changes I have experienced since I implemented CCPM which I am going to discuss in this book, I still have a hard time believing the above statement is my reality now.

When you have an unstoppable cough, you see the doctor. The doctor examines your condition. It might be a cold. It might be influenza. It might be an allergy. The doctor minutely observes your appearance, interviews you, and evaluates the symptoms in order to identify the problem. He then decides on a prescription of cough syrup for you. However, the cough is just a symptom of an underlying illness. With cough syrup your sickness is not cured, the symptoms are just suppressed. Meanwhile, your sickness might get more serious. If your sickness is diagnosed as an illness, medicine to cure that illness is needed to cure you.

Likewise, with corporate diseases, sometimes we often see only the symptoms on the surface of the problem and try to treat them. If this medicine doesn't work, we try the next new medicine, and then newly discovered "breakthrough" medicines, one after another. By doing so, the entire organization becomes overmedicated. In order to avoid this, we need to consider and understand the problem more deeply; we must search for the root cause of the problem instead of being puzzled by surface symptoms.[1]

1. I use the "Thinking Process," which is TOC's method for analyzing problems and discovering holistic solutions. It is a very easy and convenient thinking/analyzing tool, and can be harmoniously used with other management methods. In fact, in most cases, I find a synergy effect in daily practice. TOC emphasizes Win-Win thinking, so it is natural. Oops, I am talking about methods here. I might be intoxicated by them, too!

The Trap of Visibility

Various management methods are actively being developed and introduced in order to cope with these challenges. However, it is still very rare to see remarkable success in the real world.

First, let us verify the following statement:

In order to "Achieve the goal," it is necessary to "Visualize the status."[5]

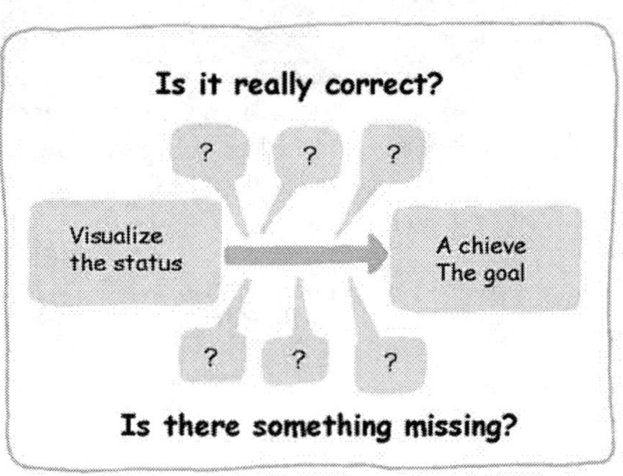

This seems to be a common sense statement, and many people would agree with it. Indeed, with the very high uncertainty and complexity of the "projects world," there is little

5. It sounds like "If you build it, he will come" from the movie *Field of Dreams*. I might believe "If you visualize the status, 'he' will come" to bring us profit. However, 'he' often came to give me more paperwork, reports, meetings, etc!

hope of success if you undertake projects without having first envisioned an ever-changing status. Now let's verify the logic in a different way:

If you "Visualize the status," you can "Achieve the goal."

Looked at this way, the statement appears to be insufficient. Even if visibility is in place, it is not always possible to achieve the goal. In other words, **"visibility" is a necessary but not sufficient condition.**[6]

The next figure will show an analysis of the situation surrounding a project.[7] Management's emphasis is on the importance of customer satisfaction. At the same time, it is necessary to increase sales as much as possible.

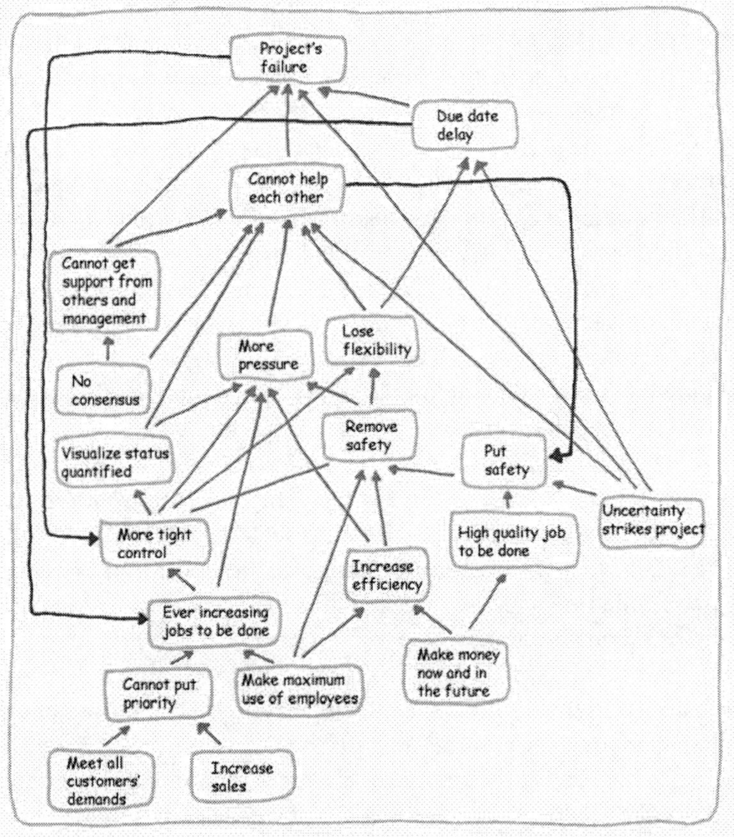

6. I really like Dr. Eli Goldratt's book, *Necessary but not Sufficient.* It was a real eye-opener for me. In math class in elementary school, I learned "necessary but not sufficient" logic, but I realized that I have not checked for sufficient conditions very often since I started my career. Rather I have used necessity logic more often as I go up the corporate ladder, which means I get more illogical as I get more experienced. This is a very sad fact that I must admit Dr. Goldratt's book reminded me of.
7. This chart is known as a current reality tree (CRT). If you want to study it more, please refer to the excellent books of Dr. Goldratt.

In such a situation it is difficult, however ideal, to give priority to each request, and this leads to a situation where there are ever-increasing jobs to be done. In order to make money now and in the future, we want to make maximum use of project members so that the most jobs are done with the highest efficiency. In order to enhance efficiency we must remove the safety from each task (to avoid project resources from standing idle). And, in order to make sure the ever-increasing jobs are done in a correct and timely manner, we need to have precise status visibility. In order to effectively monitor project progress, the visualization of project progress must be quantified. If safety is removed, and tighter controls are in place, we lose flexibility should uncertainty strike the project. Tight control, quantification of progress and ever increasing jobs create more pressure. With no safety in the project, even if a problem occurs or someone in another project is in trouble, we cannot help each other. But managers come to us to request we help them out by stressing a "sense of urgency" and "sense of teamwork," and we are eventually forced to help, even when our situation is almost as severe (as in the initial project—when we first learned the lesson that we had better increase safety for each task in the future, just in case). When management realizes project members have more safety in each task, they will remove the safety in order to increase efficiency. Meanwhile, if we cannot help each other because we have little flexibility, when uncertainty strikes a project, it causes due date delays. If the due date is delayed, the project duration gets longer, causing more opportunities for additional changes and leading to additional jobs to be done. This adds more pressure to the project. Furthermore, if the project goal is not clearly agreed upon with full consensus, and the support of management and people surrounding the project cannot be obtained, we cannot help each other when encountering trouble.

In a situation in which we cannot help each other due to little flexibility, we cannot deal appropriately with problems when they arise, causing due date delays. Since new projects need to be started immediately, in conjunction with existing projects that are behind schedule, tasks continue to increase for each project member. With little flexibility or consensus of project goal, when faced with unexpected problems (which are the nature of projects) the risk of project failure increases further. If projects continue to fail, a more strictly controlled management approach is needed to tightly regulate budget and monitor status. And on and on…

What is worth noting in this figure are the feedback loops. The failure of a project accelerates a tighter management control approach.[8] Due date delays result in increasing tasks, and because help cannot be expected, we are forced to add more safety to prepare for uncertainty. The feedback cycle of additional safety drives management to remove it more intensively. This turns into an endless downward spiral and, as time passes, the situation becomes more serious.[9]

8. In this case, management normally requests even greater visibility of the project status, and many visibility methods will be evaluated. Does this mean visibility for the sake of visibility? Does it sound effective to you?

9. Everything starts with the (good) intention of making the project better. However, it soon becomes quite the opposite. It is very well said in the old proverb that the road to hell is paved with good intentions. The situation becomes worse and worse as time goes by, since negative feed back loops get more violently

Which is More Complex?

Which of the systems depicted in this figure is more complex? Is it System A? Or is it System B? Based on the number of entities involved, System B appears to be more complex. However, if you review the figure again, with regard to solving the problems in the system, it is evident that System B is much easier (if you recognize the cause-and-effect links for each phenomenon).

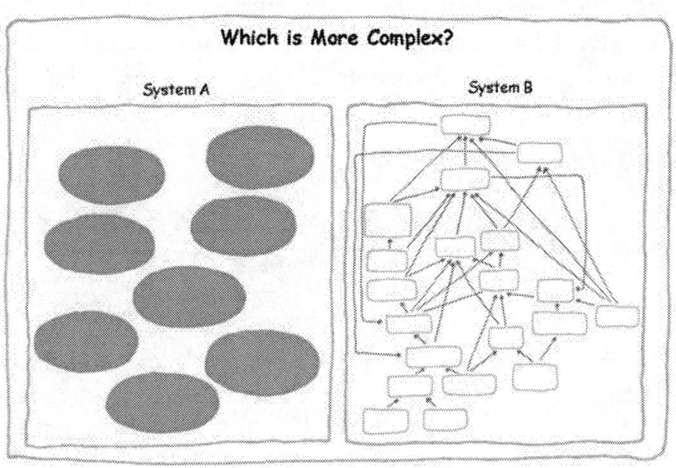

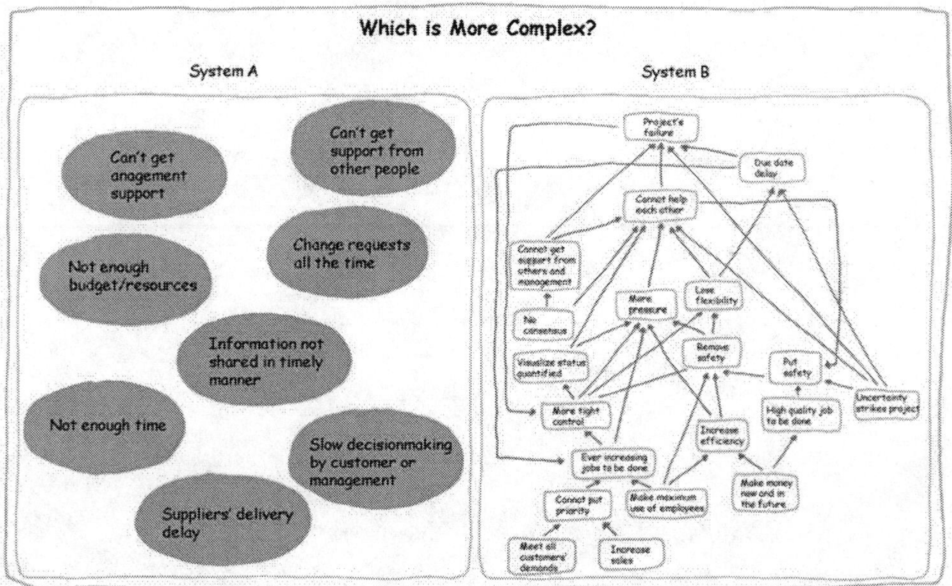

Now, let's take a look at the figure above. It reveals an insight derived from the chart above. The effects in System A are just symptoms of the problems caused by the system depicted in System B. In our daily life, we differentiate symptoms from sickness. If you have cough, you don't think the cough is a disease.[10] Instead you consider it as one

harmful to the site. I call it the trap of necessity-logic only management. It is really depressing when I talk about this to people.

10. Unfortunately, there are many company doctors (called consultants) who are trying to cure the symptoms, not the disease. Focusing on curing the symptoms might accelerate the real disease however!

of the symptoms caused by some disease and you will try to find a cure for sickness, not the symptoms. TOC takes this approach too, by analyzing problems in a systemic approach,[11] and developing the specific medicine for the specific disease. [12] TOC makes use of these links in complex systems to generate a simple yet powerful root-cause-solving solution for whole systems.

Motivated Bugs Mutated to De-motivated Bugs

Project work is supposed to be fun by nature. If you will remember, when you wrote software codes for the first time and saw that it worked, it surely gave you great pleasure. It is the same in the construction business—when you build a house for the fi rst time, it should be an unforgettable moment in your life. Projects should be fun by nature because they provide opportunities to solve new challenges, both for personal and professional growth, and people are fully motivated at first. However, this motivation is gradually lost when you continue to suffer from the command and control management that is in place.

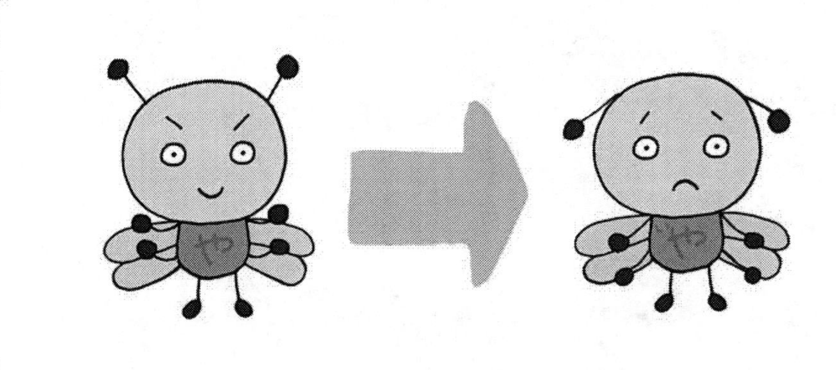

Motivated Bug mutated to De-motivated Bug.

Take a look at the two bugs—both have the same eyebrows, mouths, wings, legs, arms and feelers, only with a slight difference in angles.

11. This systemic approach is surprisingly common thinking as in the "asking 5 times why" method of Dr. Ohno's Toyota Projection System. Not being led astray by superficial symptoms, but focusing on nailing down root-cause issues is the key. Since project issues are associated with the organization, it must be analyzed from a holistic, systemic viewpoint.

12. TOC calls this specific medicine an "injection," which is really true if you see how effective it is.

Session 03 It is PEOPLE who do Management Reform

Undesirable Effects in a Project

Senior management often talks about problems with projects, such as: "Visualization of the project is a big problem;" "I don't know what's going on;" "What are the real problems happening on the site;" "Project leaders are not helping each other," and " When problems are reported, it is always too late."

On the contrary, the problem often expressed by project members is that the project seems to be a tunnel without an exit. Complaints from the project members are often, "Everything is top priority" or "I cannot understand what management is thinking." Management's support of the project team is extremely low. "Leave it to you" style management is in place, and a sense of pressure is the only impression project team members get from management. Then unexpected problems, one after another, arise for the project teams. This leads to an "ever increasing scope" and an often heard complaint that "we can not get help from management, despite the fact that we ask for it."

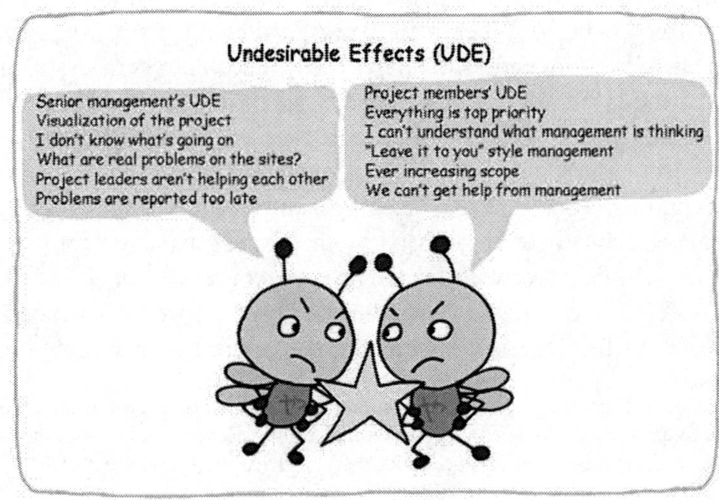

Of special concern, in most cases, is that the key members of the management reform team also have daily work to do. Thus they are placed in between a rock and a hard place—between the priority of the daily work and the project task at hand.

What Senior Management Expects of Project Teams

What does senior management expect from each project team in order to practice better management?

- -Visualize project progress accurately to see if it can meet the due date.
- -Make sure the quality of the project meets expectations.
- -Report problems before it becomes too late to take appropriate actions.
- -Achieve maximum performance with limited resources.
- -Make sure project activities are based on the corporate philosophy and are socially responsible.
- -Enhance teamwork.
- -Develop opportunities for personal and professional growth for project members.

To do the above, regular project meetings are held featuring project report presentations. However, in reality it is extremely difficult to understand the real situation correctly, to recognize and comprehend problems, and to take appropriate actions, since the amount and quality of time that senior management must devote to achieve this is quite huge.[13]

When troubled projects emerge one after another, the situation becomes more serious. It becomes necessary to manage them more precisely in order to prevent the projects from failing. To manage precisely, progress reports need to be presented in the most accurate and detailed manner possible. This is necessary in order to pick up on the problems in an early enough stage to enact appropriate countermeasures. In the meantime, project members are extremely busy. When paperwork for the projects increases, it may interrupt the progress of real project tasks. This causes more project failures to occur. In order to cope with this situation, a new project called the "Project Failure Termination Project" will be launched, which directly reports to the CEO of the company. To make sure to avoid project failure, it is necessary to visualize the progress much more precisely with intensive control of cost, time and resources, and with a more cutting edge advanced management method than ever before (led by the project management office). In order to do so, it requires more paperwork for the project progress report. At this point, project members really understand the importance of progress reports (since it is directly reported to CEO). All of the project members cooperate to stave off project failure

13. Imagine a situation where you sit in a management meetings hearing ten-minute reports from each project manager, filled with complicated jargon, for five hours. How to understand the situation? How to take actions? For me, it sounds like I'd need God-like ability to do so. Some people can do that but I can't.

through intensive paperwork. However, this leads to a situation where project members are wrapped up with ever increasing reporting and administrative work, resulting in less care for essential project tasks. With little care for essential project tasks, it naturally increases the risk of problems. But once problems occur, project members then have to concentrate on real project tasks, and project report work is stopped. Senior management loses the visibility of the project progress and then...[14]

It is People who do Projects

It goes without saying that it is *people* who execute projects. Consider the following questions:

You must do two completely different tasks this week. You have two options to do them:

> *-Focus on one task through completion, then when completed, work on the next one.*
>
> *-Do both tasks, by turns, simultaneously.*

Question 1: Which is higher in quality?
Question 2: Which is faster?

You will answer intuitively that focusing on one single task will result in higher quality and faster production. Of course! It's common sense.[15]

In corporate management practice, it is almost impossible to use unlimited resources on projects. In order to produce maximum performance with limited resources in limited time, it is natural that it is important to decide on the priorities of management.

---

14. The number one complaint in projects I hear everywhere is that there are too many meetings and excessive reporting, while number one problem in the project is often said to be lack of communication. It is quite ironic since the purpose of meetings and reports is supposed to enhance communication.
15. Here I want ask you one more question. Do you always focus one task, or do you practice multi-tasking? Oooops, you may just have realized a fact of life: "Common sense is not common practice."

Session 04 The Dilemma of Management

Everyone understands the importance of deciding on priorities. However, it is surprisingly difficult, perhaps almost impossible, to do so in daily business life. Although daily work is always a matter of top priority, that does not mean management reform is second priority at all.

Companies or organizations that have many active projects in motion exist in what is called a multi-project environment. The figure below shows the dilemma this presents for management. In order to make money now and in the future, it is necessary to increase sales. In order to increase sales, it is necessary, as much as possible, to provide many tasks for project members to complete simultaneously. Management doesn't want idle time when project members don't have anything to do, rather management wants members to do something to increase sales.

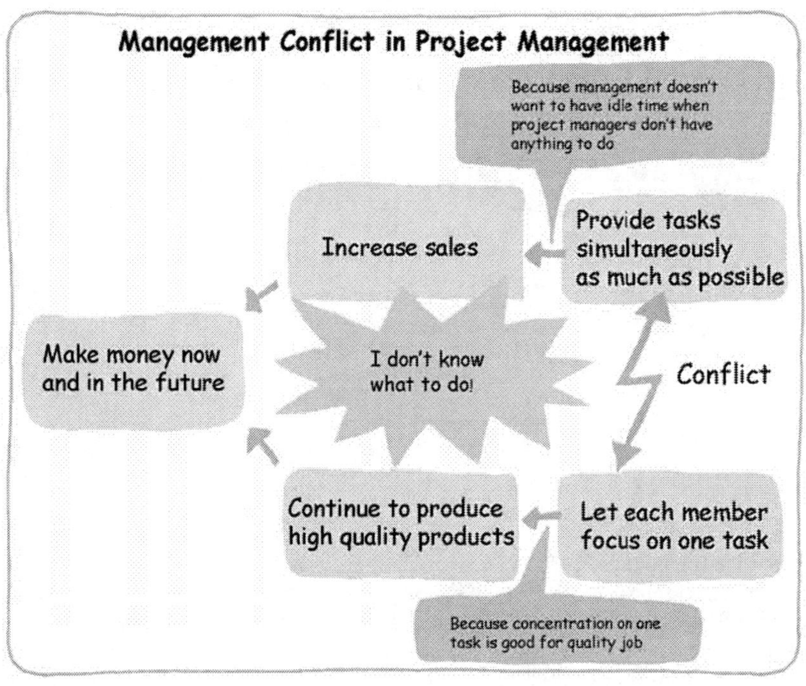

On the other hand, in order to make money now and in the future, we need to continue producing high quality products. In order to do so, it is necessary to let each project member focus on one single task at a time, because if there is a quality problem, it may lead to a big claim by customers. This will cause cost increases due to the process of settling claims, especially in terms of time wasted, which may affect the next order or market share.

Here we have a conflict.[16] In this situation there is a common goal. However, a conflict exists because there is a difference in understanding the situation, caused by the different assumptions made by each side, some of which might be based on past experience. If you can identify an invalid assumption and successfully challenge it, you may come up with a harmonious solution that both parties can agree to without having to compromise.

In this chart, both have a common goal, which is to make money now and in the future, but both have different opinions how to do it. In other words, this problem can be frankly stated as, "I don't know how to continuously increase sales, while making maximum use of project members, so that each member focuses on only one single task,[17] and the result is a quality job."

Senior Management's Reality

Generally speaking, senior management people have a lot of experience derived from being a part of various successful projects over the course of his or her life. These include breakthrough new-business project successes, as well as remarkable project successes of rebuilding unprofitable business units. These remarkably successful projects definitely lead to a senior management career path. These people have excellent talent for project management by nature, and have been practicing project management for years.

Let's look into minds of these senior management people. What would you think if they manipulated safety time (SABA in Japanese)[18] in order to keep within the promised due date and budget, and also in an effort to protect against unexpected uncertainty, which they know is the nature of the projects from when they were project managers?[19]

16. In TOC, this chart is called a "cloud." Using it, we analyze the root causes of conflict and discover win-win solutions without having to compromise.

17. Year after year, I have been saying to everybody, "Focus!" But they don't do it. I must confess that this is my fault. I will explain later why it happens.

18. "Safety" is "SABA" in Japanese. SABA is a fish name, mackerel. Mackerel swim in groups in the ocean. When fishermen catch them in nets, huge numbers are caught at once. You can count them if time allows. However, SABA is known as a type of fish that rapidly loses freshness. Therefore, fishermen count the approximate number and add several SABA to just make sure customers will not get a lower number of SABA. This is the origin of the expression of SABA. So if you say, "Are you having SABA?" it means, "Are you including safety?" By the way, SABA is a great stuff for Sushi (my favorite!)

19. I must admit I did this myself all the time. My style of project management was to obtain as many

SABA sounds bad, but projects are always uncertain by nature. A "safety net" is indispensable. With strong voices and persuasive negotiation skills, they are always successfully securing excellent resources, and extending due dates as much as possible. This allows them enough insurance to keep their promise. Without a cushion of time and resources, it is impossible to help project members if unexpected problems strike. The project succeeds because of the insurance in hands of project managers.

The senior manager who has such experience will certainly feel that current project members have enough room to work within the current project parameters. Knowing room (safety) exists, senior management will squeeze more jobs into projects because they know it is still feasible to get them done.

On the other hand, project managers know their bosses (senior management) will throw new jobs into the project, one after another, to meet customers' endlessly swelling expectations. In order to comply with these requests, they need to ensure even more safety. However, senior management will sense this hidden safety inflation by project members, and in order to make maximum use of limited resources for maximum performance, and to enhance efficiency, they will continue to increase jobs for project members. Thus, the negative feed back loop will be repeated. This seems to be what is called a "vicious cycle".

How wonderful it would be if we could stop the "vicious cycle" and work together harmoniously, with mutual trust and a spirit of teamwork among senior management, project managers and project members throughout the organization, while working toward the common goal, in order to make projects succeed one after another to a point where it helps everyone's personal and professional growth. The organization could eventually grow, supported by fully motivated people! [20]

---

resources as possible and try to extend due dates as long as possible by using my large and loud voice, emphasizing the importance of my project to senior management. I am a hard rock vocalist, which helps me a lot to do that.

20. In Part 6, I will discuss your future reality tree. I hope you like it.

Part 2 SABA – In Search of Safety

さば

Session 01 The Inseparably Deep Relationship between Safety and a Sense of Responsibility

The Place where Safety is Born

Why do people need safety?

Let's examine a hypothetical case as an example. Assume you have an urgent request from your boss. Your estimated duration for this job is 9 days at the shortest, a 50/50 estimation—but your past experience tells you it will take more than that in most cases. Do you give a 9-day estimate to your boss? Think a moment. Have you ever concentrated on one single task for as long as 9 days since you joined the company? You can definitely expect additional, unforeseen tasks during the 9 days. Furthermore, you have current on-going tasks at hand. Thinking about it this way, you understand it is quite impossible to make it happen in 9 days. You need safety time to keep the promise, so you may say "18 days for better or worse!" But do you think your boss will report in 18 days to senior management? Your boss may think, "Wait a moment. I need to check and verify it to make sure the job is done correctly up to that point; it may need some rework. Let's add 2-3 days for safety's sake." Of course, senior management has an even greater responsibility than you. He or she might need to report to the CEO on this task. In this case, if a more precise content check is required, as well as more time to rework, then you many need several days. And what happens if this due date is promised to the customer in the name of the CEO? You cannot fail to meet it by any means. Thus, a few extra days (or even weeks) are needed for the sake of safety.

Bugs in the Companies
Picture Dictionary
The Safety Bug
Safety Bugs love people's sense of responsibility. They grow rapidly, eating people's sense of responsibility for nutrition. It is said they prefer to live in the silo type organization or in the space between organizations.

Credibility in the organization becomes more important as one's responsibilities get heavier and heavier. In order to protect credibility, safety is necessary by any means. There are many good people in organizations who have a strong sense of responsibility and don't want to leave other people disappointed.

Uncertainty is the nature of the project's tasks. What will happen can't be estimated. We know from experience that safety is necessary to protect the due date and to avoid letting other people down. Safety sounds good in one light, but in reality it is fudging the numbers. In short, ***because people have a sense of responsibility, people need safety.***[21]

Safety Increases by the Rat Calculation[22]

It is necessary to increase your margin of error in relation to your individual sense of responsibility.[23] The higher you rise in the organization, the higher your level of responsibility, the more you need safety. Plus, in an organization-to-organization discussion, you need more safety because each manager has a sense of responsibility as a representative (of the organization). The more you represent the organization, and the more responsibility you have, the greater safety is required.

An overly inflated safety is intolerable in any organization. In some top-down situations ("The due date is this!"), a big voice eliminates all safety throughout the organization and project members are left at a loss, with spreading distrust. Later they will have learned from experience that the safety will be cut anyway, so they will start to increase the amount of safety even more from the very beginning. Again, the vicious cycles of increasing safety and removing safety don't stop.

How do People Work with Safety?

How do people work when there is even a little safety? People may think, "There is still time until the due date," and be slow to start the task. Then, when they are approaching the deadline, they go and "cram" to make the deadline. This is the so-called "Student Syndrome." The examination grind of school days is a typical example. At first you look at the textbook and, in a flash, estimate how long it will take to learn the material. "Well, I estimate I will be able to learn it in three days at most." However, just one day

21. Imagine if you were told by someone, "You don't have a sense of responsibility." It's the kind of insult toward your business career that you don't want to hear. Thus in order to keep your sense of responsibility, you need to have safety.

22. In Japan we have a saying about "rat calculation", meaning rats increase their numbers/multiply endlessly.

23. After joining my first company, my mother's advice was "Yuji, you are no longer a student. You must have a sense of responsibility." My first boss's advice was the same. As time went on the same advice was constantly being given to me. Thus, I naturally tended to have more and more safety.

before the exam date, you find there are only twelve hours left and you have yet to learn it. Now you really must study very hard, even staying up all night. Is this something you have only seen in students?

Bugs in the Companies Picture Dictionary
The Student Syndrome Bug
Student Syndrome Bugs don't act until the very brink of a deadline, thinking, "There is always enough time. " Serious warnings may be reported, if the syndrome infects people, they sends signals to the brain that make people feel good during the"cram"time before the deadline. With continuous infection and proliferation of student syndrome bugs, people come to want desperately to cram in the midst of pandemonium, keeping them in chronic state of overwork.

Safety will be Consumed Completely

To make matters worse, there is a phenomenon called Parkinson's Law that says people will always use the given time and budget completely. For instance, you assume that you have an entertainment budget of $1,000 for the month. You use $700 up to now, with a remaining $300 in the budget and three days left until the end of the month. What do you do with the $300? Most people will answer, "Use the $300 by the end of the month." If $300 is left, most likely you will not be appreciated for cutting costs, but instead you will be chastised by the boss because your budget estimate was wrong. On top of that, the next month your budget may be reduced to $700.

Bugs in the Companies Picture Dictionary
The Parkinson's Law Bug
Parkinson's Law Bugs use up all the time and budget given to projects. It is reported they cling to all people. It must be noted that an attempt to remove these bug are sometimes dangerous because of intense resistance and serious side effects.

This does not at all mean you are a bad person. Rather, you are person with a sense of responsibility. During the day you work very hard on sales activities, and then you work evenings in the form of business discussions with important clients over dinner. Even with this hard work, monthly sales targets are barely achieved. In this situation you might think, "If the entertainment budget is reduced, the flexibility for next month's sales activities might be drastically decreased. Moreover, taking this opportunity, our competitors might invite my clients to dinner for business discussions themselves. This is unaccept-

able. Let's think. I have a good idea! Let's spend the remaining $300 on the clients who I will target next month, then I can use up all of my budget for this month and secure next month's opportunities. It may even result in a sales order this month!" Thus, the entire budgets given is used.

Polishing the Apple

Bugs in the Companies
Picture Dictionary
The "Polishing the Apple" Bug
Polishing Apple Bugs use up the given budget and time for a better "fi nish." They are a very rare species since they look like they are working very hard superficially.

It is possible to finish a job early when you have safety. But what do you do with the remaining time? For instance, your job, which you estimated to last 18 days, is finished 3 days early. You can deliver it early because the customer wishes to get it as soon as possible. But wait a moment, if you deliver it as much as 3 days early, the customer will use all three days to thoroughly check it, and this may cause requests for more revisions. Maybe you had better use the 3 days to review it yourself for a better finish, with nicer looking illustrations, graphs, charts, etc. This may please the customer as well, and as a result, the customer may give you his next business, too. Another reason not to deliver the project early is that next time you will be asked to do the same type of task within in a shortened, 15 day time period. At this point you cannot ask for money for 18 days worth of work, and from management's point of view, it will be a big problem if the price of work is drastically reduced. Therefore, let's use the remaining 3 days for polishing apples.

Multi-tasking

It is almost impossible to concentrate on one task at a time in ordinary daily life. Business is always busy, busy, busy. Under the company slogan of putting the customer first, customer satisfaction, etc., everybody works very hard. On the other hand, the activity of the management reform project is also important. Furthermore, there is a mid-term management plan project. On top of that, the cost reduction project, as well as the lead time reduction project, are also top priorities for the company. As cross-functional teams become popular, you may be in a situation where you belong to several projects at once, and you must report to two or three different bosses across organizations. You don't want to leave any boss disappointed, because every project is very important and is a top priority for the company. You must succeed in them all, and at the same time your daily job is important as well. This accelerated increase in multi-tasking is just like a plate spinning. To make things worse, as more tasks are assigned incrementally to the busiest and the most capable persons, the workplace gradually takes to multi-tasking everywhere.

Bugs in the Companies Picture Dictionary
The Multi-tasking Bug
Multi-tasking Bugs have a big sense of responsibility and are hard workers. They continuously work on many different tasks at the same time, feeling thrilled to be dealing with a variety of different things, like trying to keep many plates spinning.
It is said that some Safety Bugs mutate again and again, finally turning into Multi-tasking Bugs.

Is Safety really a Bad Thing?

Safety seems to be a bad thing superficially, but there is a way to make use of it as leverage—an indispensable tool for the project's success.

Let's introduce it now.

A Story of a Project Village

Story by Yuji Kishira
Illustration by Mayuko Kishira

Once upon a time, there was a village called the"Project Village." In this village there were hard working bugs who shared a strong sense of responsibility.

There were always unexpected things happening in the Project Village. Storms came, things went wrong suddenly, etc...

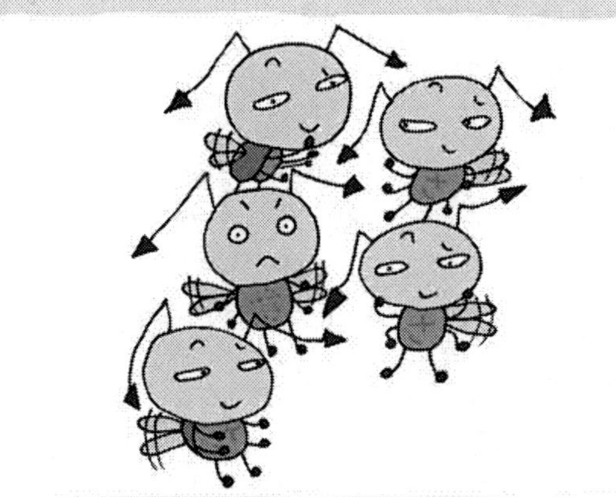

After continually experiencing unexpected problems, the bugs began to mutate one by one. The mutated bugs were called "Safety Bugs," because they hoarded safety as much as possible. Because the Safety Bugs fudged their estimates by adding safety, delivery dates started falling behind, budget overruns were common, target specifi cations were sacrificed, etc. These became big problems in the village.

A famous CCPM gas was sprayed as specific medicine designed for Safety Bugs.

We must explain!

CCPM gas was developed through the Theory of Constraints, which was invented by the physicist Dr. Eli Goldratt. This gas is a breakthrough medicine specifically targeted to solve all of the problem behaviors in a project environment.

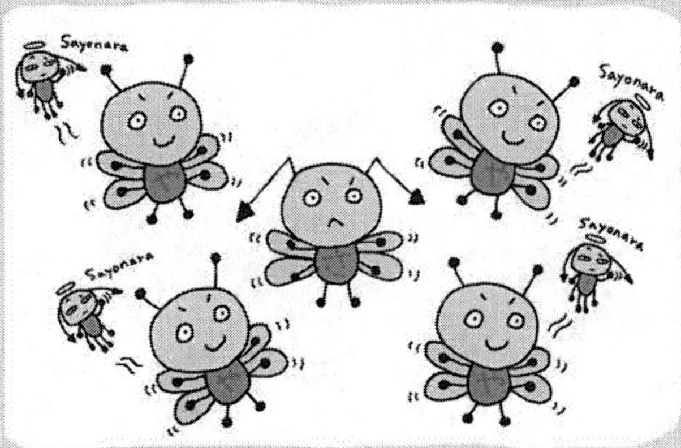

Wow! "Safety Bugs" mutated immediately into "Motivated Bugs." However, there was one bug that was different from all the others.

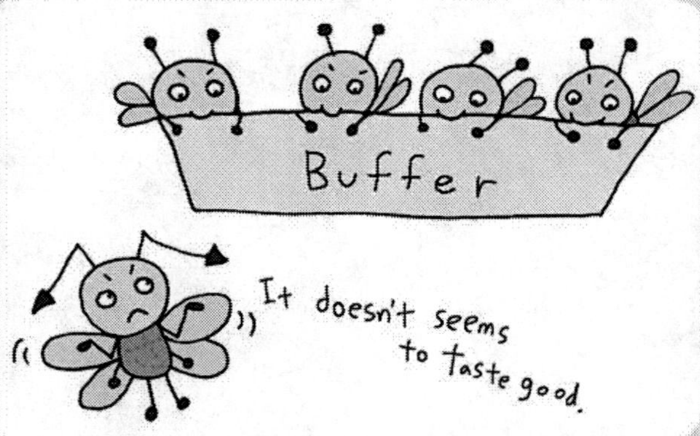

This bug was different because it didn't eat the "Buffer"* that the other bugs were enjoying so much. And though this bug didn't eat anything, it strangely did not become thin.

*CCPM's Project Buffer

Careful, elaborate research revealed that this bug still kept hidden safety which it ate in secret. This, it was called the "Hidden Safety Bug."

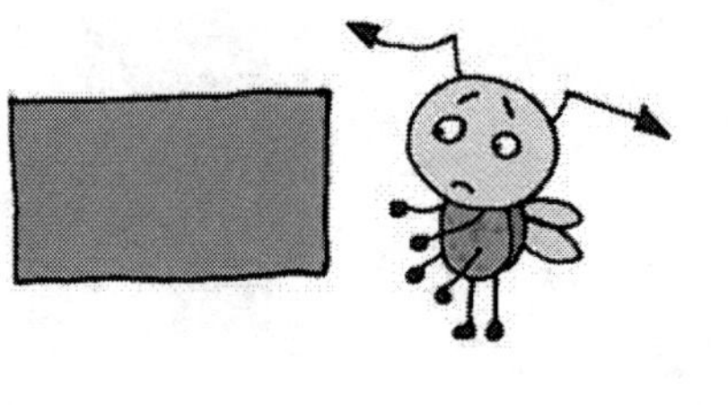

An experimental diet treatment was tried on the Hidden Safety Bug. The hidden safety was completely remove so that it could not be eaten.

The Hidden Safety Bug became thin in a moment.

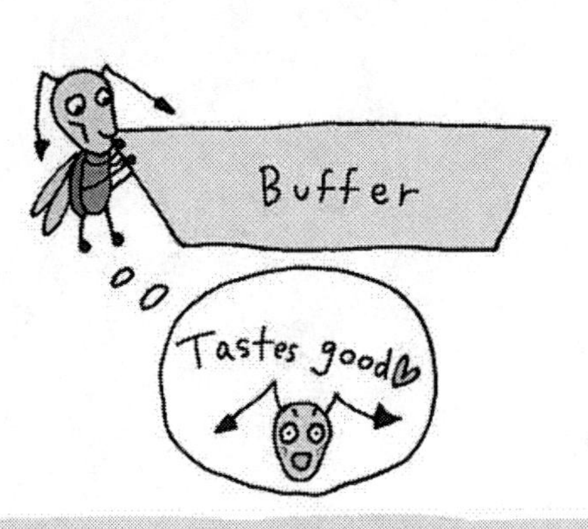

The Hidden Safety Bug then decided to eat a little Buffer and found it surprisingly delicious.

Then the Hidden Safety Bug suddenly mutated into a "Super Motivated Bug." He was called this because he developed a very strong sense of responsibility.

Super Motivated Bugs became popular everywhere. Since their sense of responsibility was much stronger, they cared about everyone's troubles. There were no more delivery dates falling behind, or budget overruns, or the target specification sacrifices. The Project Village prospered forever more.

Happy, happy ending!

Part 3 How to Use the Safety

Session 01 Is Safety always Bad?

Conflict over Safety

Manipulating the safety sounds bad in general. If safety is always bad, it should be taken away completely. However, without safety, what happens to your project?

- -Your job gets tight.
- -Should you have a problem, there is no room to take action to solve it.
- -You cannot help other project members when they are in trouble.

If your boss instructs you to help other team members, and you are already overwhelmed by so many tasks, without safety in hand you may want to say, "I need the help!" Since nobody has the flexibility to help one another, your job is increasingly tight. You cannot care about other people because you are overwhelmed with your own tasks. Tension, irritation and loss of teamwork are everywhere in your workplace, and your job gradually becomes painful.

Is safety really bad? I want to confirm this reality again.

- -If the project itself is something you have never done before, its nature is one of uncertainty. You need safety to cope with it.
- -If you have a responsibility to a due date and budget, safety is definitely necessary to ensure you keep your promise.

Both seem right in day-to-day reality.

It is becoming more and more clear that there is a major conflict in whether to remove safety or to have safety. The following figure shows this conflict. In order to make money now and in the future, you need more jobs to be done. In order to get more jobs done, you need to remove safety from the task durations, since it maximizes efficiency of the operation (effective use of members). In general, it is believed that safety deteriorates maximum use of project resources and operational efficiency. On the other hand, in order to make money now and in the future, you must maintain that a good quality job be done. In order to get more quality jobs done, you need to have safety, as the project is uncertain in nature and unpredictable things happen all the time.[24]

So, how much time do you need as safety? How do you estimate task duration correctly? If you start such a discussion, it tends to become a serious, tense discussion using many so-called three-character scientific methods.

Let me be straightforward. If the project is something you have never done before, do you really believe there can be a "correct" estimation? Before getting into such a difficult discussion, are there any ways to resolve this conflict without compromise, keeping safety and doing quality jobs that will make money now and in the future?

Capable Persons Know how to Have and Use Safety

Now I want to ask you a question. Have you ever had a tough boss who was hard on you when you were green? You might have hated him or her so much that you never wanted to see his or her face. However, years later, maybe you think of him or her with respect and say, "I was trained hard at the time, therefore I am." The tough boss, who most people are afraid of, is often said to be the person who most people admire as a depend-

24. When I was one of the project leaders, I liked safety very much because it was a secret of why I was consistently successful. However, the higher I went up on the corporate ladder, I gradually came to hate it because I believed it deteriorated the efficiency of my organization. I realized I came to deny the one thing that I had once admired as the secret of my success. The world is complicated…

able, respectable manager. In general, what a tough boss requests of you is meeting a tight due date. Take, for example, the following conversation:

> **Boss :** Have the report completed by next week.
> **Subordinate:** That is impossible, I need at least four weeks.
> **Boss :** No way! There's more than enough time for anyone to do it. You must think of how to get it done faster.
> **Subordinate**: I need three weeks then.
> **Boss:** No, no more than two weeks. If I were to do it, I could finish in far less than two weeks.
> **Subordinate:** Well, could you please teach me how to do it?
> **Boss:** No, I won't tell you. Ask your supervisor, he has done it before. Two weeks, okay?
> **Subordinate:** I will try.

When you remove safety, people's behavior becomes more desirable

For this subordinate, this job is his first experience. Since the subordinate has never done it before, the uncertainty is very high. The subordinate cannot estimate what is going to happen. Because the uncertainty is very high, safety is necessary. Therefore, it is in the subordinate's interest to manipulate the safety. However, in this conversation, the boss successfully persuaded the subordinate to reduce the safety and do it within two weeks. What happened here is this:

➔ The tight due date request convinced the subordinate it was impossible to manage the project in his or her own way.
➔ The subordinate started to learn from others to comply with the tight due date request.

When the subordinate must do the job within a tight due date, he or she will not only learn how to do it from senior people, but also will make every effort to search for KAIZEN (improvement actions in Japanese) everyday to meet the tight due date.

On the other hand, if this subordinate was left to do the same job in four weeks, with as much safety as he or she originally wanted, it would be done in his or her own way, as solely his or her responsibility. The subordinate would do it with a lot of effort, however with less experience, and when checking the progress just before due date, the situation might occur where the boss exclaims: "Why is progress so poor? You were told to always report anything before it was too late! How many times have I told you the importance of SENTE KANRI (Take action before it's too late)!" The subordinate, while working very hard, had only his or her own efforts to rely on.

However, the above situation could turn out quite the opposite were the subordinate assigned a tight due date. This is because he or she knows it is impossible to make it happen in his or her own way. Thus, he or she will ask senior, more experienced people how to do it. Senior people feel much better when they teach, instruct or train people, than when they have to force them to learn. This way it is much easier to transfer knowledge developed by years of experience in an organization to less experienced people, and the transferred knowledge will be of much higher intensity.

More than that, the uncertainty of this task will be dramatically reduced. Over the course of this intense discussion, which transfers years of past experience and knowledge of the organization, the uncertainty of the task is decreased.

Good, instinctive bosses are commonly tough,[25] since they know these things intuitively. Because of this, for your professional and personal growth, and in an effort to transfer knowledge (polished by years of experience), and to reduce the uncertainly of the project and increase the success rate of all projects, they request a tight due date of you![26]

25. Tough but tender. The tough boss is tough now but tender in the future, if you realize it. In fact, I had several tough bosses who I hated very much, but I now admire and respect, saying, "They were tough, therefore I am."

26. There are many excellent project managers who lead many difficult projects to success. I have observed hundreds of them and am convinced that there is common know-how throughout Japan, which is hidden in their favorite cliché: SURIAWASE, DANDORI HACHIBU, SENTE KANRI and YUTORI. Unfortunately, I have never met even one person who can explain how to do these. They say these are key lessons we need to learn for project success, but they can only be learned by years of experience at the sites. It seems like typical, implicit knowledge we sometimes call (in Ninja words) "GOKUI"—secret key lessons only transferred to trained persons after years of experience.

Session 02 Revealing Hidden Safety

Creating Focus on the Task while Avoiding Multi-tasking

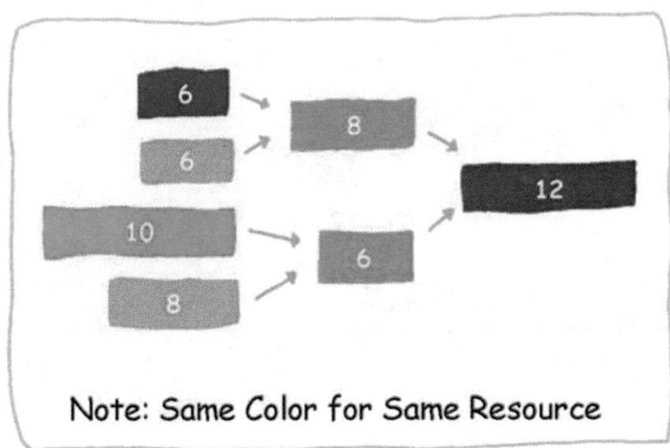

Let's look at this chart as an example. The longest path is 30 days. Let's assume you are assigned to the blue tasks. Of course, you don't want to multi-task. It is common sense that you do a far better job if you focus on one single task at a time. Unfortunately, common sense is not common practice in the real world. With big pressure from the market due to tough competition, your project must be completed within 30 days. But, if your tasks are shifted so that you can focus on one task at a time, the project duration will be extended by 6 days to 36 days. Your boss is obviously not happy at all. Your boss may think that a day does not consist of 8 hours, but 24, that a week does have not 5 days, it has 7.[27] Only by working 6 days, 16 hours each, is it theoretically possible to do these tasks simultaneously and meet the 30 day requirement. Then, your boss will negotiate with you to accept the conditions by offering a potential bonus and/or vacation time. You may say yes or no. But if you say no, you might expect a more intense discussion with your boss about potential rewards, or a philosophical[28] discussion about such concepts as the spirit of teamwork, a sense of urgency, a sense of responsibility and so on, which you are used to hearing everyday and everywhere around you.[29]

27. I like the Beatles song *Eight Days a Week,* but not for the workplace…

28. They are called sometimes the "carrot and stick"

29. There are many posters in the office showing corporate slogans, corporate philosophy, teamwork, etc… Some people told me that these were things that they didn't do: If they were doing them, there would be no reason to put them on the wall. It sounds convincing to me…

You may agree to do two tasks simultaneously but, most probably, you will give your boss one condition, such as, "Please let me focus on these tasks within this duration."[30] Your boss will most likely accept it. This is a typical discussion in the planning phase.

Due to a tight schedule, you must really consider how to proceed with these two tasks in order to complete them by the due date. Of course, you will not be multi-tasking because you know it only deteriorates your efficiency and the quality of your work. If you run after two hares, you will catch neither. In other words, you would never plan to do these tasks, a bit of one and then a bit of another, in turns. It is common sense.

So, your boss has successfully convinced you to work on two tasks simultaneously. But then he begins to worry about their progress, because he or she convinced you to accept both tasks and knows you must be multi-tasking. Because of this your boss will want to repeatedly check the status of your tasks. Your boss will come to you asking, "What is the status of the 8-day task? What about the 6-day task?" If you had been focusing on only one task, it means you didn't work on the other. That means there will be no progress at all on one or the other of the tasks. It makes your boss much more worried and concerned, and forces your boss to more intensively monitor the status.[31] This bothers you too much to concentrate on one task, and forces you to work on the other task simultaneously after all (to avoid interference from your boss). This is what we call "multi-tasking."[32]

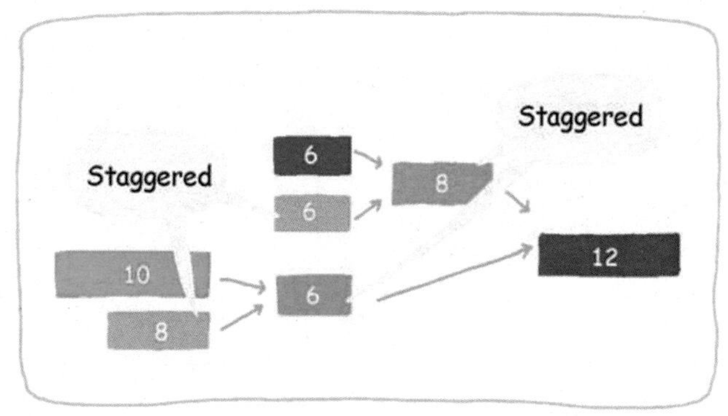

In order to avoid multi-tasking, the 8-day task and the 6-day task should be staggered. Then you can concentrate on one task at a time, and your job quality and speed are much enhanced. However, 30 days must then be extended to 36 days, which is unacceptable to your boss and the customer.

30. I received many complaints that two tasks at a time were not common: three, four, or five at a time are much more common in daily practice.

31. I want you to notice that your boss has good intentions, but he believes he needs to monitor the status in order to keep the due date. He thinks this even more since he asked for two tasks simultaneously. When we analyze corporate problems, most of them are caused by good intentions, the desire to make things better, but they have quite the opposite effect. That's sad.

32. Your boss considers you to be a capable and dependable person, thus you are trusted to make a plan for the tasks. In general, project members are smart and are believed to have the competence to make plans effectively. Your boss believes this since you know the tasks better than him. However, in the execution phase, the story is completely different. Since you were trusted in the planning stage, your boss now doesn't know the details of your plan; he will intensively monitor the status because of worry, which means your boss might *not* trust you. It's very interesting to see how your boss's trust differs between the planning and the execution phases.

Enhance Job Quality in the Task by Building Teamwork

Taking a careful look at this chart, you can identify the longest chain, called the "Critical Chain,[33]" on which you need to focus your attention in order to reduce the project lead time.[34] The "Critical Chain" identified below is the chain consisting of the 10-day, 6-day, 8-day and 12-day tasks. Looking first at the 10-day task, there must be safety involved, since people have a sense of responsibility to meet a due date. In a previous conversation between the boss and the subordinate, the boss successfully convinced the subordinate to accept 2 weeks instead of the original estimation of 4 weeks. But in most of the cases, this is very difficult to achieve unless you are an experienced and powerful person. However, there is a much easier way to remove the safety from the task, which is ***to give a 50% buffer to the task duration as long as an "aggressive but possible" (ABP) estimate is given***. An example of the discussion is as follows:

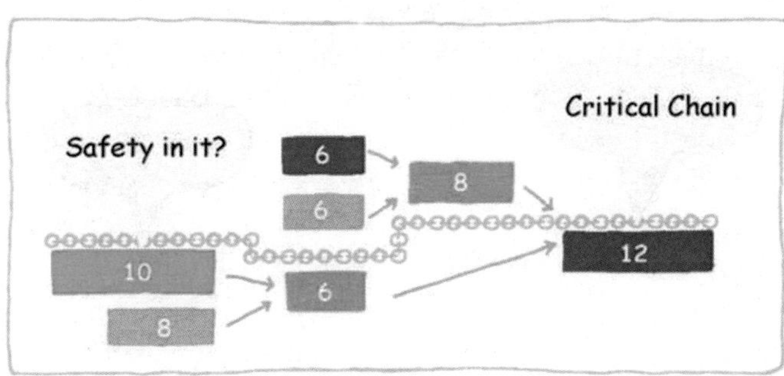

> **Boss:** 10 days? Don't you think that is too long? (He is wondering, is there any safety included? If you have a sense of responsibility, then there must be some safety. This leads to the next question.) "Do you have sense of responsibility?"
> **Subordinate:** Of course I do.
> **Boss:** Then you must have safety built into the 10-day task, right?
> **Subordinate:** 10 days is really aggressive since there is such great uncertainty in this task.
> **Boss:** I'll tell you what, how about 7 days as a challenge lead time? You don't have to promise 7 days, but just consider 7 days as a challenge. If you say it is necessary, I will give you 3.5 days as a buffer, which is half of 7 days. In other words, there won't be any penalty for lateness until 10.5 days, which is longer than 10 days.
> **Subordinate:** No penalty until 10.5 days? Really? Then I prefer to take 10.5 days. By the way, if I finish within 7 days, can we have a vacation for 3.5 days? Our team will be excited about it.

33. This method is known as Critical Chain Project Management (CCPM), which was invented by Dr. Eliyahu M. Goldratt. I strongly recommend reading "Critical Chain", published by The North River Press, to understand more details.

34. The term "critical chain" was coined because it is different from "critical path", which did not have resource conflict consideration. However, in PMBOK Issue 3, critical path also takes resource conflict into consideration. So, technically they look the same, however I think critical chain has more human-centric scheduling logic.

Boss: Of course you can. However, I must remind you that you must be entirely completed in 7 days in order to take the vacation for 3.5 days.
Subordinate: Well, I'll need to discuss how to do it in detail with team members, but I am sure that the members will be highly motivated if I offer 3.5 days vacation as long as the team finishes it within 7 days. If we finish it, we would like to go on a spa vacation as a team. We must arrange travel plans now with the travel agency.
Boss: Are you sure? If the team target is 7 days, it is possible it will be delayed if you seriously consider the uncertainty that you just talked about. I want to remind you there is great uncertainty in this task, as you have just now told me.
Subordinate: I believe our team is going to target 5 days internally to make sure it happens within 7.
Boss: All right. How can I help you to make it within 5 days? I think we can really make this happen.
Subordinate: Wow! You are so nice. Boss, would you participate in our planning meeting? I want you to share your experience and knowledge with our team members, so that we can make a very good plan.

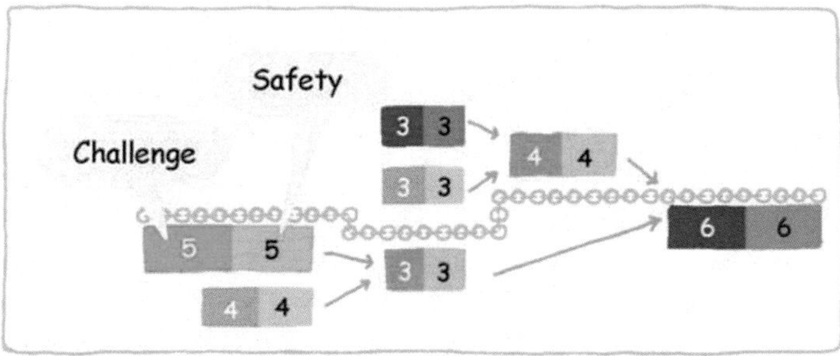

As a result of the above discussion, each task will be broken down into two parts: an "aggressive but possible" challenge lead time and "safety." It is recommended to have a discussion among team members involving experienced senior people. Through this conversation, the knowledge and experience of senior people within the organization are transferred to a younger generation easily and naturally.

Although it seems to be only a slight change of scheduling, it brings about a dramatic change in the behaviors of project members.

In the case of a task duration of 10 days (including hidden safety), if the task members face unexpected troubles (which are the nature of projects), they will work hard to fix them by using their own safety, since they all share a sense of responsibility to complete the task within 10 days. They will use maximum effort to do it. However, if the troubles are beyond their capability, then they will report them to the boss and discuss how to deal with them. Normally, this problem is reported to the boss at the last moment, when they are already approaching the end-of-task due date and it's too late to take action.[35]

35. Why always at the last moment? It is very simple. It is just logic. Since project members have their own safety, which is also their source of responsibility, they naturally try to manage any uncertainty using

They say, "Boss, we have been working very hard at this task but the progress is currently delayed due to unexpected problems. We may need a few days to complete it." The boss may reply by saying, "Why did you leave the problems for so long and report them too late to take action? I have been repeatedly telling you that you must report them as soon as possible, before it becomes too late! How many times do I need to tell you the importance of SENTE KANRI?!"

However, in case of a 5-day challenge target, with 5 days safety, the story will be completely different. With a 5-day challenge target, members expecting a potential 5 day vacation if everything goes well have much greater motivation to complete the task within 5 days, far ahead of normal. Also, members will more deliberately prepare tasks before starting them, by involving experienced senior people. Should any unexpected problems arise, they will be reported immediately to members, and to the boss (since they won't diminish vacations[36]), and they will work on corrective actions, with a team effort, as soon as possible. Why a team effort? It is very natural, because the safety is originally coming from a sense of responsibility. If you share the safety among the team, you naturally share the responsibility among the team. This is what we call "teamwork". In other words, **the safety, when it is shared, is transformed into the source of teamwork.**[37]

Feeding Chains to Protect the Critical Chain

We must also be aware of one more thing. If the tasks that make up the feeding chains, which are merged into the critical chain, are delayed, it will extend the critical chain schedule. In order to avoid this, you can do that the same thing to the tasks on the feeding chains. Thus, task members will have a shared sense of responsibility, and teamwork will protect the critical chain from delays on a feeding chain.

Holistic Decision Making Enhanced through Teamwork

Uncertainty is the nature of projects. It is not uncommon for the scope of projects to increase, through the addition of tasks, due to unexpected reasons. Project members might think these increases are inconsequential, especially considering their future relationship with customers (they are repeatedly told to consider customer satisfaction). In cases where they have safety, they are willing to accept new tasks as a local decision, for corporate policy mandates customer satisfaction. Of course, it is a very good thing to make the customer happy. It is common that project members want to make the customer

their own safety (sense of responsibility).

36. In this discussion, vacation works like "carrots" in the project.

37. Many times I have heard my boss stressing the importance of teamwork. I knew it was important but it was very difficult to build. However, now I know that just by sharing safety together, teamwork will be built. It is much, much easier and practical, without pain at the sites.

happy more than anyone else, since they sometimes are in direct communication with them. However, it may not necessarily be good from a holistic view of the whole project. A small additional change, for the sake of customers' happiness, might cause serious problems down the road, especially if there had been other more important requests that were initially dropped by management due to the tightness of the requested due date.

On the other hand, with an "aggressive but possible" challenge duration, the story will be different. Project members cannot accept additional tasks at the local level, because they don't have their own (individual) safety anymore. Any additional request will be reported to the boss immediately (where the safety is managed for the whole), to see whether it can be accepted or not. Since the safety (which equals responsibility) exists at the whole project level, the decision will be made in terms of a holistic view of the project.

Providing Concentration for Project Members

A tight task duration is also good for project members. Management knows that project members are working very hard to complete tasks with an "aggressive but possible" 50/50 task duration. So in this situation, even senior management cannot easily add additional tasks to projects, since they know that project progress will be delayed because of it. If additional tasks are incorporated, it becomes very clear that any delay caused will be management's responsibility, not the project members'. Therefore, any changes will be more carefully reviewed by management and involve project members, creating a holistic perspective. The project members then understand the importance of how each task is linked with the project goal from management's point of view.

Building Trust throughout the Organization

This also provides a very good working environment for team members to concentrate on the assigned tasks, which they understand are more tightly linked with management goal, and they get more support from management, therefore enhancing trust throughout the organization. Projects are uncertain by nature, so people need safety. However, when it is hidden, it may create distrust towards each other. **The safety, once shown and shared, can be utilized as a source of teamwork.[38] This is the starting point for building trust throughout the organization.**

38. Sharing safety means sharing responsibility—which means teamwork, doesn't it?

Safety Bug Maxim: Steal Experience with your Eyes

It is one of the most common maxims that experienced project managers use at the sites. It is believed that it is the best way to transfer experience and knowledge to the younger generation. By watching the old-timers, the younger generation will comprehend their meaning and practice of "thinking." It is great method; the only issue is that it takes too long.

Session 03 Where the Safety Should be Located

Creating Teamwork in the Project

Once you know what safety is, and that when it is shared it is the source of teamwork, it becomes very easy to build teamwork at the project level. Then it is only necessary to gather all of the discrete, task-level safeties into one place, which means the project team now shares the safety and the sense of responsibility of each task. In other words, all responsibilities become one, now shared among the team, and it is called "teamwork." This shared safety is known as a *project buffer.* It protects the due date from the uncertainty of the project.

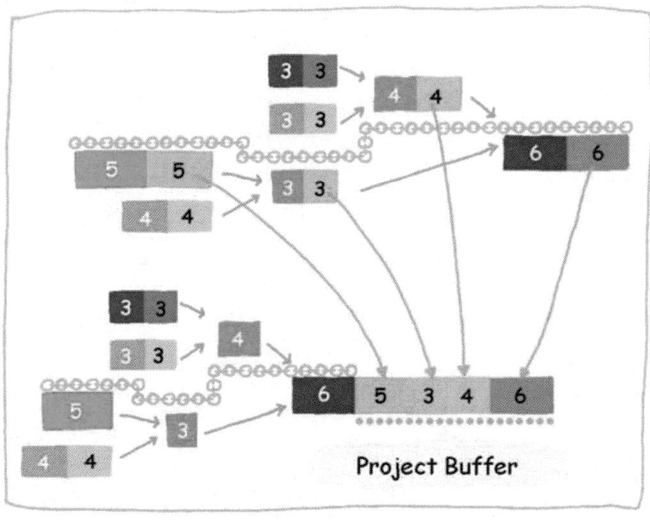

The members of an individual task on the critical chain don't have their own safety, so they must concentrate on one task seriously, without any allowance to take on additional tasks that might cause multi-tasking. The members of the next task are anxiously waiting to start on their upcoming tasks, like a relay runner anxiously waiting for the baton passing.[39] The tasks on the critical chain are really activated in

39. In *Toyota Production System* (Productivity Press) Dr. Taiichi Ohnoalso stressed the importance of the relay runner ethic. As I go deeper into learning TOC, I have come to more deeply admire the beauty of Toyota Production System.

a sequence, just like one single chain of tasks with an "aggressive but possible" challenge duration, and a project buffer at the end so that project manager and members can protect the due date from uncertainty.

The Teamwork Ethic Depends upon the Location of the Safety

Now it becomes very clear in this figure whether to have or to remove safety. If there is safety in an individual task, it allows those members to play individually, and you or your team must carry the responsibility alone. But if it is shared among task members, it builds teamwork at the task level. Once it is shared among project members, it builds teamwork throughout[40]. **So, rather than having individual safety, let's have shared safety if you want to build teamwork!**

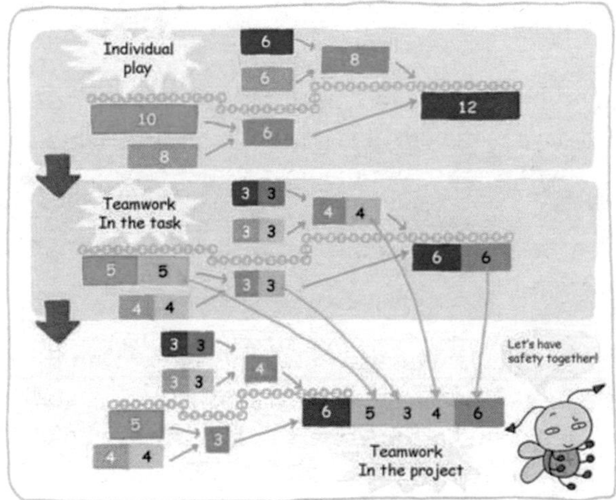

40. There is a case study at the end of this book titled: "Win-Win-Win public works reform." This case study taught me a great lesson, where when a small local construction company started to show their buffer status in public, it built the teamwork among the construction company, government officials and taxpayers (local residents) with a shared common goal. It was the society-level teamwork that surprised me a lot.

Session 04 Buffer Size

Give the Appropriate Safety in the Project while Keeping Appropriate Tension among the Members

Please take a look at the previous figure. It shows:

- "Aggressive but possible" challenge task duration of 5 + 3 + 4 + 6 = 18 days
- Safety duration of 5 + 3 + 4 + 6 = 18 days

Don't you intuitively think there is too much safety? If your boss forces everybody to do the task within 18 days, while he or she keeps the same safety of 18 days duration, it is natural that people will want to use the boss's safety as much as possible. Are there any ways to estimate an appropriate buffer size, to keep the due date safe and secure, while maintaining tension among the project members? The answer here is a simple mathematical calculation.

Please take a look at the first 5-day task. What is the probability that it will be completed within 5 days? We estimated a 50/50 task duration probability. This means there is a 50% chance to complete it within 5 days. How about the chance of *not* completing it within 5 days? It will also be 50%. In this case, a safety of 5 days is calculated. What is the probability that you will use this 5-day buffer? It will be 50%. How about the next, 3- day task? The chance of completing it within 3 days is 50%. The chance of not completing it within 3 days is also 50%. So the chance of using the buffer of 3 days is 50%. Thus the chance of four buffers being utilized is 50%.

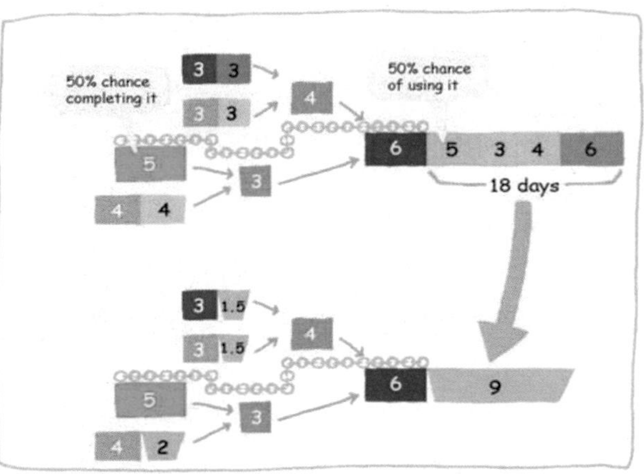

It means it can be calculated:

$$(5 + 3 + 4 + 6) \text{ X } 50\% = 9 \text{ days}$$

Buffer Size = Management Decision

However, this is just a mathematical calculation to establish a reference point. It is recommended to set a buffer size based on management's decision. Projects have uncertainty by nature and, because of a strong sense of responsibility, project managers, leaders and members want to have as much safety as possible in order to keep a due date. However, with a longer buffer, the project duration will be extended. In the case of most projects, a customer's payment comes after project completion, so cash accordingly comes later. During a project, a company must ensure cash flow, in order to pay everybody's salary, resources, etc. It is management's responsibility to protect this cash flow. Thus, buffer sizing should be management's decision.

Start Tasks as Late as Possible

In general, projects have long durations. The longer a project becomes, the more the associated uncertainty increases. The uncertainty comes not only from the internal organization, but also from the external world (that is beyond our control), such as the rise of unexpected competitors, unexpected economic and environmental changes, etc. The longer the duration becomes, the more the risk is increased. Therefore, the earlier you start tasks, the more you increase the chance of being exposed to unexpected uncertainty.

It is not uncommon for projects to be forced to start all over again due to market and/or environmental changes. Unfortunately, it is the reality of these projects that once they have begun, it is difficult to restart them from the beginning. However, while people naturally want to utilize some of the deliverables that have been generated so far, it may cause more extra tasks than if they were to start again from scratch.

Bugs in the Companies
Picture Dictionary
The Money-eating Bug
Money-eating Bugs emerge where there is too much safety, consuming excess resources and budget. It is often observed in big companies affected by the "Big Enterprise Disease".

Moreover, the longer the project duration becomes, the higher the probability that new projects will be required to start, increasing the number of ongoing projects and further adding to the uncertainty of existing projects. This situation exhausts resources throughout the organization, and forces it to utilize outside resources, rapidly consuming the company's cash flow.

All projects have their due dates. As long as you can maintain the due dates safely, it is natural to start tasks as late as possible, thereby decreasing risks. If you start earlier than necessary, the project has more time to be exposed to uncertainty. In other words, by starting tasks as late as possible, while observing market and/or environmental changes, you can reduce risk. Once a project gets started, it should be completed as soon as possible. This is the most practical way to manage projects—to reduce the potential risks along the way.

The project plan discussed here is one way—removing the safety from individual tasks and sharing it among the team— is one way to help each other achieve completion as soon as possible. With this project plan, as long as you make sure there is the buffer to protect due date from uncertainty, there is a higher chance of meeting the due date.

The Critical Chain as People's Chain of Teamwork

Please compare the two schedules below. The upper schedule shows 36 days, while the lower one shows 27 days. You might prefer to have a longer duration in general. However, if you look at the details in the upper schedule, each task has hidden safety, and task members will work very hard to meet the due date by using their own safety through their own efforts. Since they have their own safety to cope with the uncertainty, they tend to deal with it in their own way, with their own sense of responsibility, and any delays tend to be reported too late. In most cases, problems are reported to the boss at the last moment, very close to the due date, and the boss gets upset, screaming, "Why didn't you report this much earlier? I have told you many times that you must report problems as soon as possible!" Contrary to this situation, the lower schedule shows how all project members are highly motivated, sharing knowledge and experience, and members of the next task are anxiously awaiting the previous task's completion (just like a relay runner's baton).

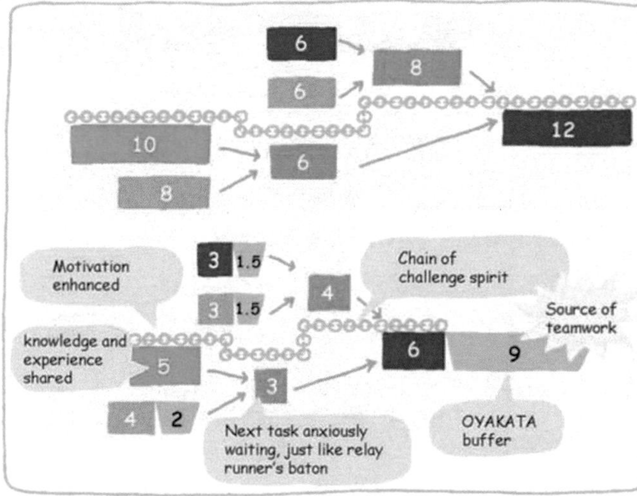

Here they enjoy a spirit of a challenging "aggressive but possible" duration for each task, with the buffer placed as YUTORI at the end of the chain to protect the due date from uncertainty (which is also source of teamwork among all project members). Which of these two situations would you prefer to have as a project leader? The choice should be obvious, since the lower schedule has management logic

Is this new to us? Not quite. In our minds, we intuitively manage projects as in the lower schedule, since we know, of course, it is PEOPLE who do the project. Whenever I create a schedule like this, it reminds me of the beauty of the spirit of "WA", which means harmony, peaceful, sum and Japanese.

A Story of Worrying Bugs

Story by Yuji Kishira
Illustration by Mayuko Kishira

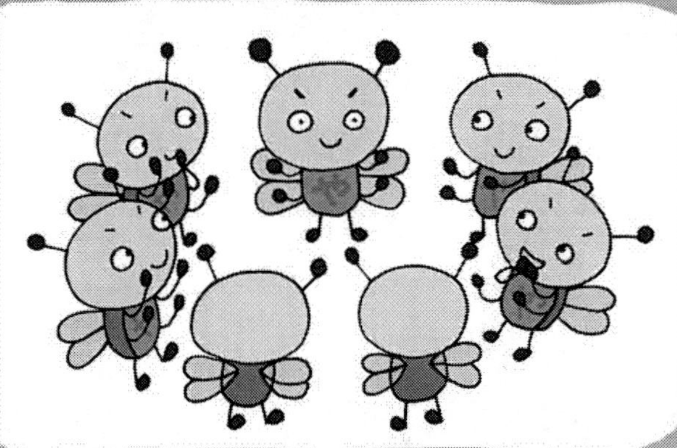

Once upon a time, there were "Super Motivated Bugs" in the Project Village. Any time there were problems, the Super Motivated Bugs immediately got involved and solved them, one after another. One bug, having sympathy and diligence like no other, enjoyed a very dependable reputation that earned everyone's trust.

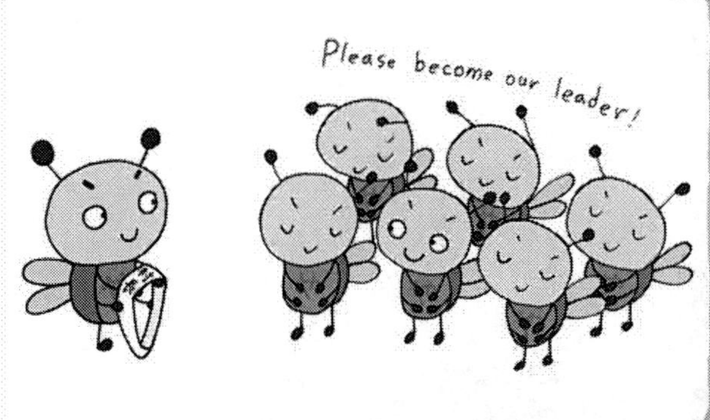
Please become our leader!

One day he was asked to become a village chief. He decided to accept for the good of the village, but he had mixed feelings since he would have to leave a project site that he liked a lot.

However, a little while after becoming a village chief, he became more and more anxious. He could no longer understand what was going on at the project sites. In the past, he could detect potential problems with his sharp senses of feel and smell,and take action far before it became too late. However, far from the project sites, neither his feelers nor his sense of smell were useful anymore. "If it were me, I would do it differently..." He continued to become more and more anxious, worrying very much.

He was determined not to be defeated. He searched for solutions, and he found out there were a lot of management methods available to solve his problem. Deciding immediately to introduce several methods, he thought everything should be pretty much in control soon.

However, things just got more and more frustrating.
Even though work schedules and progress were quantified and clearly visible, the site situations became more and more foggy. There was great a difference between the figures shown in the reports and the reality of the sites.The village chief grew increasingly irritated and more worried..

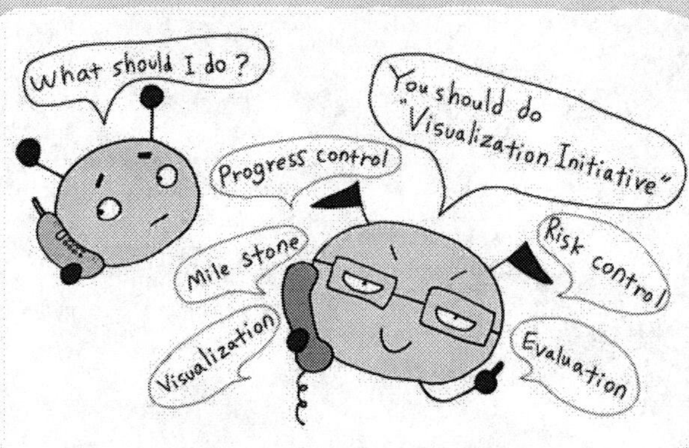

The village chief decided to consult with a famous "Should Bug" who had a reputation for knowing all kinds of management methods. The Should Bug said, "You should concentrate even more on the visibility of of all activities. There are all kinds of methods to improve the visibility of the project."
Since the chief's reliable sense of feel and smell did not work anymore, the only sense he could rely on was "sight." So he agreed to put more focus on visibility. All the cutting edge methods he knew of were implemented. It should be okay now, he thought..

Increased visibility would surely be effective. All status and progress was reported in greater and greater detail. However, because the sites' problems were now being reported in even greater detail, rather than evaporating, his frustration grew even worse. "What's happening here? Why are there still problems? Why do we ignore them until it is too late?" The number of meetings drastically increased in order to discuss all of the detailed issues.

At the same time, the sites were getting more panicked and confused. With increasing status reporting, paperwork and meetings, the time to do essential project tasks was drastically reduced. "It has become more difficult to do our job since he became a new village chief." He used to have a good reputation as a most dependable boss. Now, everybody was starting to dislike him.

One morning, the village chief noticed some changes in his body. Some of his feet had transformed into a calculator, magnifying glass, carrot, and stick. He began to quibble with every insignificant detail.
He had become a "Worrying Bug."

Although he became proficient at digging out details, calculating numbers and manipulating the carrot and stick, he continued to get more worried. And the more he worried, the more everybody fudged the count so that he didn't have to worry. They added "safety" to their estimates. The more he used the calculator and the magnifying glass, the more everyone fudged the count. The more he used the carrot and stick, the more everyone lost the sense of helping each other. "Safety Bugs" were everywhere in the sites now...

One day, he found a news item about the new CCPM gas, specially developed for multi-project organizations. "Once, I was cured by CCPM gas. If there is a new type for multiple projects, it might be good for my organization." He decided to give it a try.

Immediately after spraying the gas, everyone returned to being "Motivated Bugs" with surprising speed.

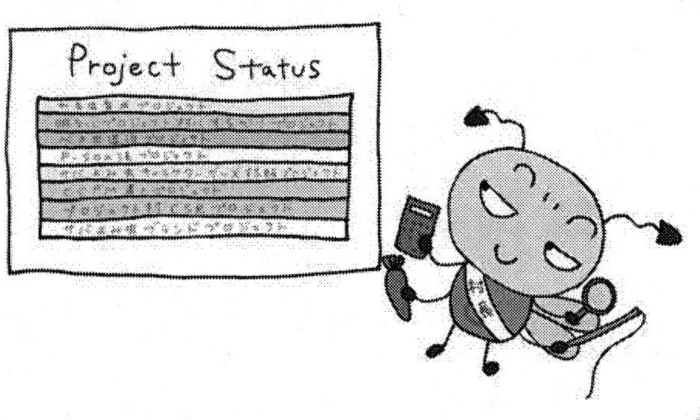

It was now possible to see the real status of all projects in one view, without a magnifying glass or calculator. He did not have to worry when a project's status was green. When yellow appeared it was possible to prepare action. And when the signals turned red, everybody started to help each other. Soon everyone naturally began to help each other whenever there were problems. The village became more fun and cheerful. He felt as if he had retuned to what he used to be as a Super Motivated Bug and he no longer quibbled with insignificant details...

One morning, he noticed his calculator, magnifying glass, carrot, and stick had come off his feet. Instead, a fan with illustrations of green, yellow and red hearts was attached to his left hand.* He had become "Comfortable Bug."

*In Japan,
a fan in the left hand means,
"No worries, relax, comfortable."

Everyday was a happy day, with everyone smiling and helping one another. It was like playing for fun, but all projects progressed with a new, almost unbelievable speed. Moreover, everybody started evolving into Super Motivated Bugs.
The village became very famous, attracted many visitors, and prospered indefinitely

Happy, happy ending!

Part 4 Remaining Duration

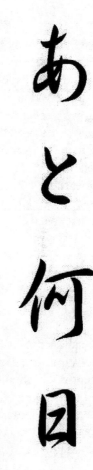

Session 01 The Myth of Progress Reporting

90% Completed!

Please take a look the figure below. It shows 90% completion of a project. This can be translated superficially as it is almost finished. However, a voice inside may tell you, based on past experience, "The remaining 10% will be a real challenge, since usually it is when the due date approaches that the deliverables get more clearly visualized, and you can expect more revisions from customers, sales, marketing, etcetera." Also, this could be translated that you have used 90% of your project budget. In this case your inside voice may tell you, "Spending money is not necessarily approaching the goal." Spending 90% of the budget creates earned value, but it might also be earned risk—if there are unexpected troubles at the final stage of the project causing rework for the most of the work-in-progress (which has probably happened in your past experience).

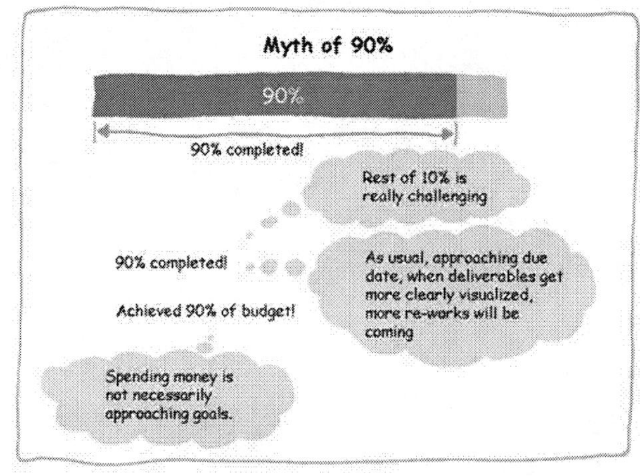

A Japanese proverb says, "If you want to go one hundred miles, ninety miles should be considered half of your trip." In fact, I have met hundreds of project managers who say from the point of 90% completion, it takes almost the same time duration to reach 100%. "There's many a slip 'twixt the cup and the lip." This proverb still holds true today.

It goes without saying that it is people who execute projects. Of course, if you are evaluated by the rate of progress, you will behave in a way that will *show progress*. Although, if you expect to need some revisions at the final stage, consumption of 90% of the budget equals 90% progress of the project.

An Easy and Simple Cure

There is a very easy yet powerful solution for this situation. Simply ask:

"How many working days remain until you are done with this task?"

I have two simple questions for you. First, when do you think you can estimate the task duration more correctly?

A. Before starting the task
B. After starting the task

Of course the answer will be B, "after starting the task," because you know the task content better.

The next question: When do you think you can estimate the task duration even more correctly?

A. 3 days after starting
B. 4 days after starting

Again, the answer will be B, "4 days after starting."

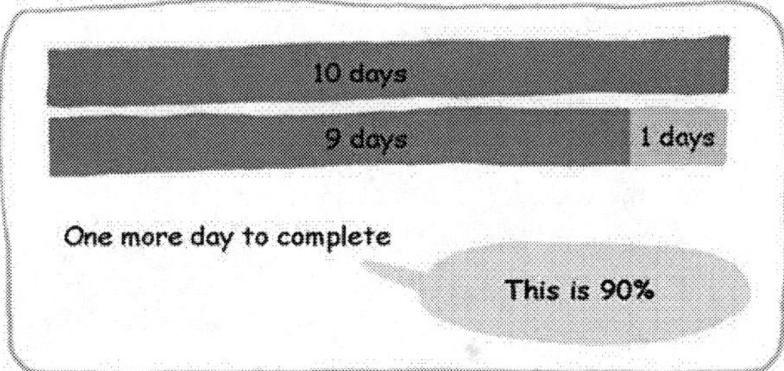

What would you think if the task manager tells you, 9 days after starting, "I will complete it in one more day, by tomorrow."

It sounds like a very accurate estimation, and can be considered 90% progress. Because a project, by nature, involves uncertainty, if you continue asking for the remaining estimated duration, the estimation will be progressively more accurate as time goes by.

Personnel Growth

Asking for the remaining duration is also a simple but powerful tool for personnel training. By simply asking for the remaining duration, a sense of keeping a deadline among project members will be cultivated, since they will pay more attention to the due date in order to keep their promise. Also, it helps to train the project members in project duration estimation, which is one of the hardest parts of project education. This simple daily question from the project leader will consistently train members to estimate the remaining task duration. With an accelerated, shared sense of keeping a deadline, it drives members to consider a better preparatory plan, while enhancing the quality of the job.

The Pitfall of Progress Rates

Now let's take a look at this figure. For a 10-day task duration, after 5 days, your estimated remaining task duration is 7 days. What percentage do you report to your project manager?

A. 50% since you spent 5 days and want 5 days' salary
B. 30% since your progress is only 3 day's amount of task
C. 5/12=41.6666666%, which is mathematically correct

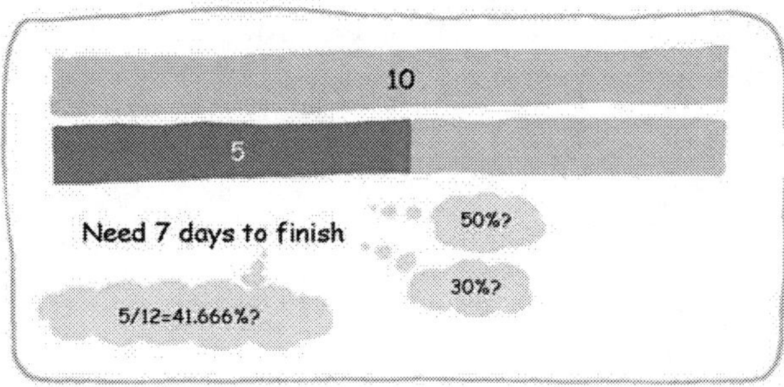

Sorry! All are wrong, because my question was wrong.

I have to remind you of the objective of progress management. It is not to make a progress rate report, but to *manage* to keep the due date! To that end, a 7-day remaining duration means that you will miss the due date by 2 days. But, fortunately, you know that now rather than later, and you can take countermeasures to reduce 7 days to 5 days and keep your promise. This is SENTE KANRI, where you *manage* to take action before it is too late.

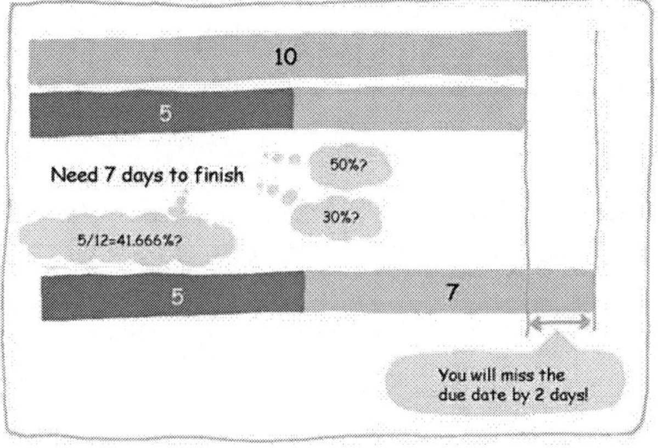

This is not new at all. I have one more simple question for you. When you are one day before the due date, do you discuss the project status by percentage, such as 98% or 99%? No, you discuss it in terms of, "Only one day left to complete!" It is very natural—common sense and common practice in your daily life.

Session 02 Buffer Management

SENTE KANRI just by Checking Buffer Consumption

Now it becomes very easy to manage progress—you simply monitor buffer consumption. For example, please refer to the chart to the left—it shows a 6-day task followed by a 4-day task, where they are estimated with a 50/50 "aggressive but possible" duration. The buffer duration is 5 days, which half of the 6-day + 4-day tasks.

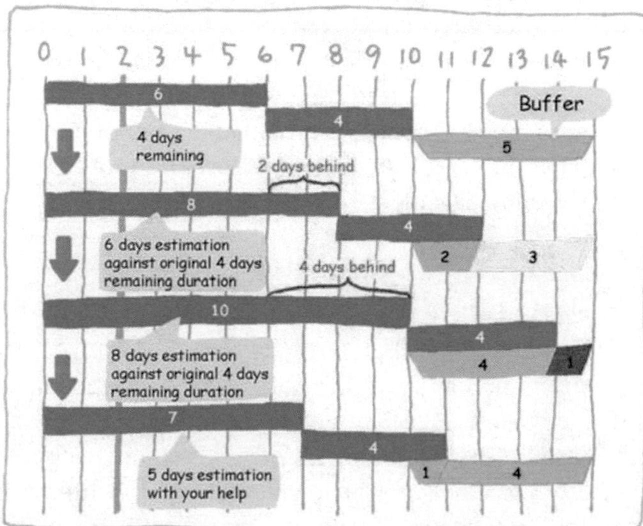

At 2 days after starting the first task, you have discovered this task is much more difficult than expected, and you estimate that you still need 6 days to complete it. The initial task duration will be extended by two days, and the next, 4-day task is pushed out by two days. As 2 days' buffer is consumed out of the 5 days, the buffer signal turns yellow.[41] Upon further evaluation of the status, you might discover the situation is much

41. Critical Chain software shows buffer color changing according to the consumption of the buffer. You can set when the signal of buffer color will be changed.

worse than previously thought, and you will need 8 more days to complete the initial task. This pushes out the second task by 4 days, consuming 4 of the 5 days of buffer, and turning the buffer signal red.

What would you think, in this situation, if the project leader reports that this project will be finished on time, and is maybe even expecting to finish one day prior to the due date. It may really be true, because the figure clearly shows it will be completed by the 14th day, still leaving a one-day buffer. In fact, the project leader may well understand that the situation is critical, but after working two days on the initial task, he or she may have a better understanding of the content of the project, and with a big sense of responsibility, he or she decides to work very hard to complete it on time. Can you trust that you will finish on time? Or do you feel worried?

There is a different way to comprehend the status on the exact same chart. By only the 2nd day of the project, which is the very initial stage, the remaining buffer is at one day, since the initial task has already consumed as much as 4 days out of the entire 5-day buffer.

Which do you feel is right? Of course your intuition tells you that the latter one is right. It is correct, I think, if your objective for progress management is to keep the due date. I don't think you would leave the situation as is, rather you would go to discuss with the project leader and other members how to take countermeasures to recover such a big delay at the very initial stage of the project. In fact, since it is only the 2nd day of the project duration, there is still a great deal of flexibility with which to enact some countermeasures. You may come up with a new idea to complete the initial task within 5 days, which is only one day behind the original estimate. Then it will pull back the second task by 3 days, showing the buffer consumption reduced from 4 days to 1 day, resulting in a green signal; "A stitch in time saves nine." This way, you can take action far before the due date is in jeopardy, which we call SENTE KANRI. The mechanism of SENTE KANRI is now embedded in your project management.

Let's Talk about the Future instead of the Past

If you start the remaining duration discussion as a part of daily progress management, you may notice a small but significant change; all of the project members are now discussing the future, rather than the past. In traditional management, you are supposed receive a report of what they *did* (in the past tense), which is not necessarily linked to keeping the due date as promised. Instead you are now discussing the estimated duration to the due date and your actions in the future tense, which is much more effective in keeping the promised due date. It is natural to discuss your future actions if you want to keep the due date, rather than your past actions.[42] In fact, it is not exaggerating to say

42. The past actions are also supposed to be effective as excuses for project delay, but in most of the cases in my life, my bosses were never happy at all.

that the only information required to keep your promise is what project members are going to do for the remaining duration, that is, the future. Since this discussion naturally directs all members' attention to the future, it will enhance members' motivation with a keen understanding of the due date and teamwork, created by the shared buffer. You can change the future, but not the past.

Without Safety, you Cannot Help Each Other

Uncertainty is the nature of projects. Common sense says that even the deliberately simulated plan, with an array of risk estimations, cannot completely eliminate uncertainty. In order to cope with it, safety is by all means necessary. Without safety you cannot help each other. Thus, safety, which is a buffer, becomes the source from which to help each other. Everybody emphasizes the importance of a spirit of teamwork. If you really want to have the spirit with which to help each other in your organization, it is necessary to have safety.

MYK (Mirai Yochi Kunren) = Risk-anticipation Training

There is a very good method for anticipating risk. It is asking the question:

"What problems, if any, do you anticipate in completing this task?"

The most important thing to know when keeping a due date is what you are going to do until project completion. Uncertainty is the nature of the project, but you can estimate risks as the project advances, and your risk estimation will become more accurate as you have a better understanding of the project parameters. So, it is recommended that after you have the answer to *"How many working days remain until you are done with this task?"* you ask, *"What problems, if any, do you anticipate in completing this task?"*[43]

This question leads people to consider/simulate the potential risks to their tasks through completion. If there are any, it is a good opportunity to take preventative countermeasures to nip them in the bud. This is also a good chance for project members to enhance communication throughout the team, and help them to learn from experienced people how to avoid risks. Prevention is better than a cure.

43. Don't ask the question "Are there any problems?" This question leads often people to answer "No problem." By the way, "No problem" in Japanese is Mondai Nai. It sounds like Monday night, doesn't it?

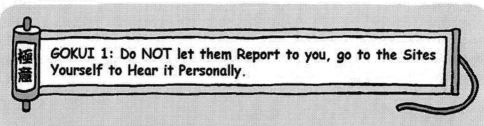

GOKUI 1: Do NOT let them Report to you, go to the Sites Yourself to Hear it Personally.

Progress reports should not be reported by project members, instead project leaders should go to the sites (GENBA in Japanese) to hear it directly. Excellent Japanese managers respect and practice 3 GEN policies, which are GENCHI (on the site), GENBUTSU (real things), and GENJITSU (reality). Project leaders ask, "How many working days remain until you are done with this task?" Then they ask, "What problems, if any, do you anticipate in completing this task? " It is commonly said that communication is the most important part of the project. This discussion provides a great and valuable opportunity for the project leader to communicate with project members, avoiding potential risks and helping them in a timely manner. On the contrary, if you leave project members to report to you, you only see the results of the progress, and your countermeasures tend to be too late. The responsibility of the project leader is not to monitor project progress, but to manage the project to success. In order to do so, the most important task for the project leader is to communicate with project members. The project leader, by asking these two questions, utilizes the most valuable opportunity to lead the project to success and practices the 3 GEN policies.

The Buffer Protects Members, Leaders, Managers and Senior Managers

It may seem that an "aggressive but possible" task duration causes big pressure for project members, but that is not true. In fact, it is quite the opposite. It protects them. While the buffer is green, project members, the project leader and senior management don't have to pay attention to it in too much detail, and project members can concentrate on their tasks. They no longer bother with miscellaneous reporting paperwork, and can just focus on the task at hand (as long as they report the remaining duration).

Since the task estimation is an "aggressive but possible challenge duration," it is natural to consume some buffer. This is because if the task estimation is a 50% chance of completion, there is also a 50% chance of not completing it in time. By just monitoring the buffer consumption, project leaders, members, and senior managers can take actions before it is too late.[44] In other words, by promising a challenging lead time, project members will be rewarded by getting a desirable working environment from management, where they can focus on their tasks (as long as buffer is green), and receive management support far before it is too late and the buffer turns to yellow and red.

44. In critical chain, it is recommended that managers let project members focus on the tasks in green, managers prepare countermeasures in yellow, and execute countermeasures in red. It is designed not to bother project members and rather to provide environment to focus on the tasks.

In fact, even if the buffer turns to yellow or red, it does not mean the project has missed the due date yet. It is just showing one of the potential scenarios of the future. It allows you to take action to restore the buffer far before it becomes too late.

The "Feeling" of the Buffer

When the buffer is green, members can focus on the tasks at hand with a secure feeling, since they know green is safe. If it turns yellow, your boss will start to ask questions about what kind of help you need to recover from the delay, and you feel safe since you know your boss is preparing countermeasures as a recovery plan to help you out. Even if it turns red, your boss will take the countermeasures that are prepared beforehand, turning the buffer color from red to green or yellow, where you feel safe and secure. If the buffer alarm is reported long before it becomes too late, and the project still fails, it is management's responsibility of course. Thus, a mechanism is now in place where the responsibility is automatically shifted to upper management.

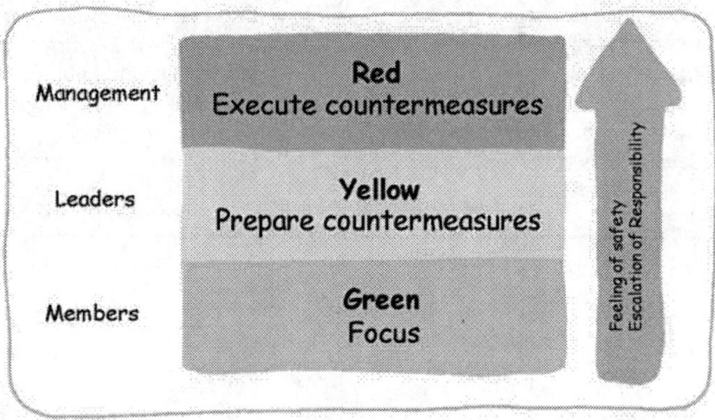

極意
GOKUI 2: Change Ceremony Meeting to Meeting

It is commonly said that these two questions: "How many working days remain until you are done with this task?" and "What problems, if any, do you anticipate in completing this task?" change the meeting dramatically. Traditional progress reports tells you what has happened in the past, which is not necessarily linked to the objectives for the meeting. This is true even for reports that are very detailed and rich. The more complicated the reports, the harder it is for people to understand, and this means it will get much more difficult to communicate. Everybody agrees on the importance of communication, since it is people who do the projects. It is especially true that most projects involve ordinary people. These two questions are a very simple but powerful solution so that everybody practices communication during the meeting. The goal of the meeting is for the people to communicate—to discuss and help each other—by sharing the status, ideas and information for better project performance.

Some people have said to me, "In the past there were so many long meetings, or should I call them ceremonies, with a variety of reports, but with no evident conclusions and no positive effects. But now meeting for just one hour is good enough.
We have enhanced communication and have experienced a dramatic change with cheerful discussion, helping each other and building widespread trust across the organization. Moreover, I have begun to look forward to the meetings in order to meet people and help each other."

Show the Buffer

Sometimes, you suffer problems from outside the project and it is believed to be out of the project members' control. However, there is a good and easy way to handle this—just show the buffer to the outside parties. If you present the buffer to the people who are delaying your tasks, it shows them clearly consuming it. The more slowly they take action, the more the buffer is consumed. They also have a sense of responsibility, recognizing that the project is being delayed because of them, and they will immediately support you. Why? It is natural behavior. As you remember, the buffer originally comes from a sense of responsibility and is the source of teamwork if shared. So, when it is shared with them, it naturally creates teamwork with them.

Where it has been implemented throughout Japan, it is quite interesting to see how the buffer is now creating teamwork, providing a good environment in which to concentrate on tasks, and allowing SENTE KANRI to help each other. Some people have said to me that it is just like going back to the good old days, extending "showing-the-belly" type trust throughout the organization.

Is it late because
of me?

To create teamwork

To concentrate on the tasks

To allow SENTE KANRI

Building "show-the-belly" trust

Session 03 Provide Buffer Visibility Across Departments

The Buffer is the YUTORI (composure) of your Mind

What is happening when the buffer status of all of projects across the organization are visualized together? In the case below, the buffers are now shared among all departments throughout the company. As discussed before, when project members share the buffer, it is the source of teamwork. Now the buffers are a source of teamwork across all of the organization, since all of the departments share them.

This figure shows an example of the buffer status across the organization, and is quite similar to the one that I experienced a few weeks after our multi-project implementation. It was quite surprising for me to see all of the project leaders begin caring about other projects. Although the project leader with a red buffer did not ask for help, other leaders fervidly started to discuss how to help his project, and offered various types of support to help it recover. I asked them why everybody started to care for each other. The answer was interesting. "Uncertainty is the nature of projects. It is inevitable for everybody. It is natural to help the project with a red buffer, if my buffer is green. Then, in the future, the project leader who is helped this time will help me when my project has a red buffer."

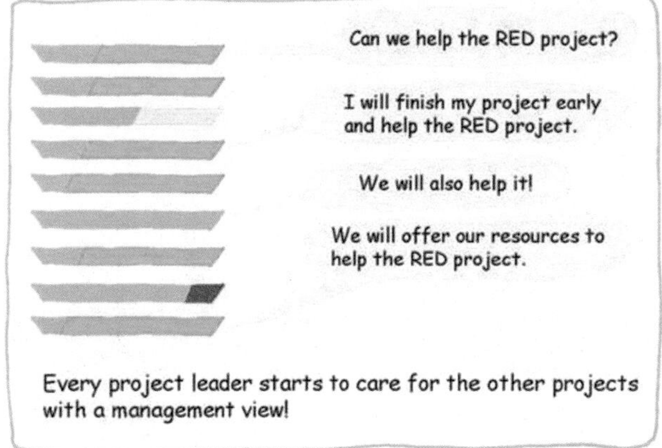

Can we help the RED project?
I will finish my project early and help the RED project.
We will also help it!
We will offer our resources to help the RED project.
Every project leader starts to care for the other projects with a management view!

"Helping each other" and "teamwork" are morals that we are repeatedly taught since childhood. On top of that, "Respect WA (harmony)" is something that all Japanese know, since it is the very first sentence of the first Japanese constitution, generated in 604AD. It is an amazing fact that the shared buffer naturally drives WA throughout the organization.

Recently, the question I most frequently ask people is, "When do you feel that you are working at a good company?" Most answer, "I feel my company is a good company when I am helped out in cases where I'm in trouble." Nothing is more appreciated than when other people help you when you get into trouble. And you remember it, offering help to them in return when they get in trouble. If there is YUTORI (composure in English), which is a buffer, you can help others. Without a buffer, you cannot help each other. Thus, the buffer is YUTORI of mind to help each other. On top of that, it helps personal growth. Since project members are trained daily to make decisions from holistic points of view, in other words, from the management viewpoint, it helps them to become good managers in the future. Spreading teamwork, accelerating personnel growth and enhancing management support with growing trust throughout the organization will naturally come harmoniously.

Autonomic Visualization vs. Visualization

Please look at the previous chart once again. Do you think there is any difference in understanding between project members and senior management? I don't think so. Everybody throughout the organization shares the same understanding of project status, and the priorities of the holistic organization, and project members freely and autonomously help each other in order to make things better for the whole organization. It is quite obvious to everybody.

Dr. Ohno stressed the importance of autonomic nervous systems in the business organization:

> *"In our production plant, an autonomic nerve means making judgments autonomously at the lowest possible level."*[45]

It can be said that the buffer is just like KANBAN, which makes it possible to make judgments autonomously at the lowest possible level.

Sometimes *visualization* creates more trouble at the sites, spreading pain throughout the organization, because it does not consider the autonomic nervous system. In a traditional environment, most visualization comes from the results report, which reports what happened on the site in the past. At the point at which the results report is made to the senior management (or I should call it the brain), everything becomes part of the past, and it is too late to take action. However, autonomic visualization makes it possible to make judgments autonomously at the lowest possible level where problems occur. This means problems can be taken care of immediately at the sites, as long as project members have the same understanding as senior management. It can be said that **autonomic KAIZEN needs to bring the brain to the lowest possible level,** where problems should be taken care of before turning into results. This is in contrast to most visualization,

45. *Toyota Projection System,* Taiichi Ohno, Productivity Press ,P45.

which brings reports of what happens on the shop floors to the highest management level for a decision (when it is usually too late, since it is always reporting a result—what happened in the past). Although it is very difficult to bring the brain to the lowest possible level, because of the challenge of developing a nervous system where it is assured that judgment is no different between senior management and workshop members, once it is successfully developed, visualization is much more effective because it is autonomic visualization.[46]

Create YUTORI to Manage it

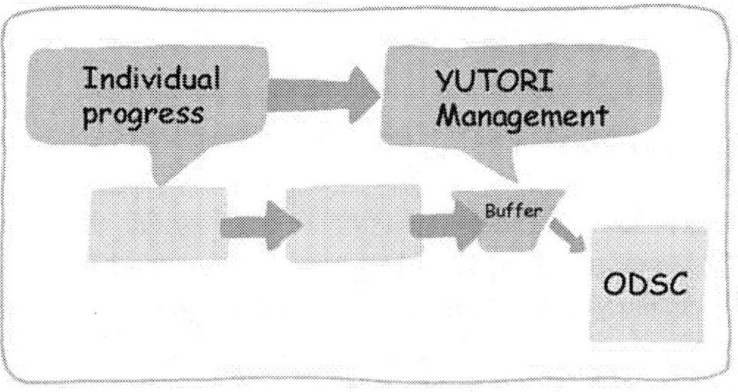

The buffer is safety, or in another sense, YUTORI. We collect the individual safety of each task to create one YUTORI and we manage it. In traditional project management your focus is on the progress of each task toward completion, while in this case your focus is on the YUTORI in order to manage all projects to success. If you remind everyone that it is people who do projects, managing YUTORI is much more comfortable to people's minds.

Here, the conflict between "have safety" and "remove safety" is dissolved. There is a good way to have safety, and you can use it effectively for management if it is placed at the appropriate location. This makes it possible to do SENTE KANRI, enhance teamwork and generate trust throughout the organization with the WA spirit.

46. Some senior managers at Toyota told me, "You must be very careful about the word 'visualization.' Visualization alone is very easy but not necessarily effective, since you must go to senior management to make decisions, and when you do that, it is too late. Real visualization must be 'autonomic visualization' which is much harder to do." It was quite amazing that Dr. Goldratt made possible an easy way for people like me to do it.

A Story of the "Can't do" Brothers

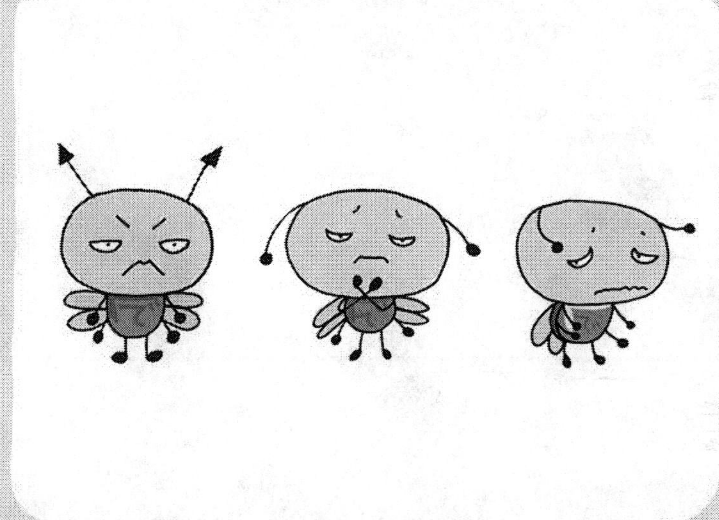

Story by Yuji Kishira
Illustration by Mayuko Kishira

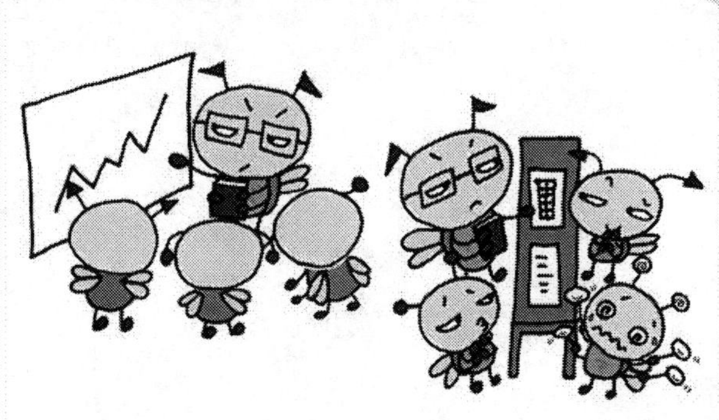

Once upon a time, there was a village called "Methods." Methods were very important there, and everyone was always studying new ones.

One day, "Comfortable Bug"came to the village to introduce CCPM, which had recently been getting very popular.

The"Can't do"brothers, who were famous in the village for having all kinds of knowledge, said: "We know all the good things about CCPM, but we don't think we can do it in this village."

Here we must introduce the "Can't do" brothers. They are: "Special Can't do Bug,"the eldest; "Complex Can't do Bug"the middle, and"Uncertain Can't do Bug," the youngest.

Comfortable Bug questioned Special Can't do Bug.

Comfortable Bug questioned Complex Can't do Bug.

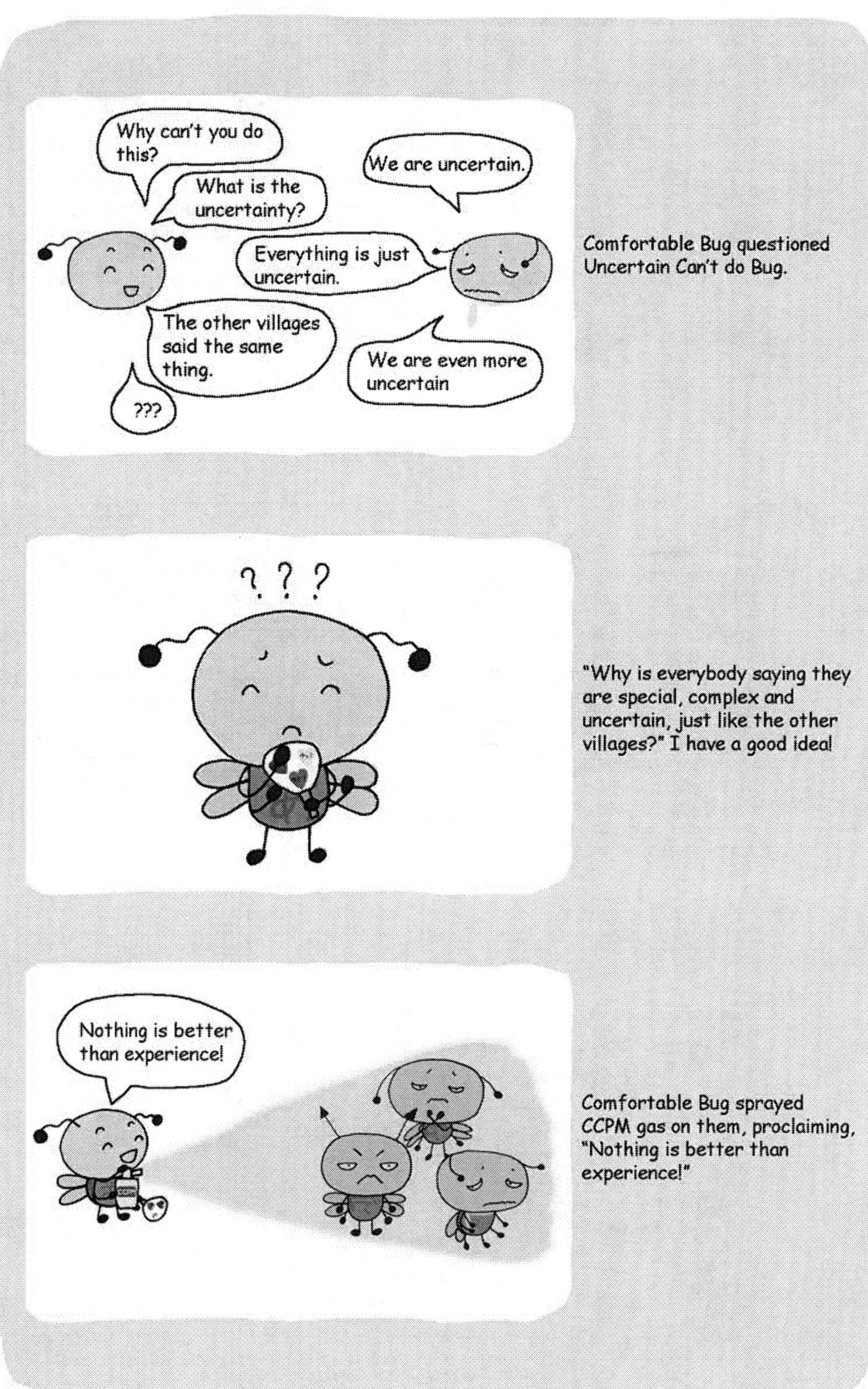
Why can't you do this?
What is the uncertainty?
We are uncertain.
Everything is just uncertain.
The other villages said the same thing.
We are even more uncertain
???
Comfortable Bug questioned Uncertain Can't do Bug.
? ? ?
"Why is everybody saying they are special, complex and uncertain, just like the other villages?" I have a good idea!
Nothing is better than experience!
Comfortable Bug sprayed CCPM gas on them, proclaiming, "Nothing is better than experience!"

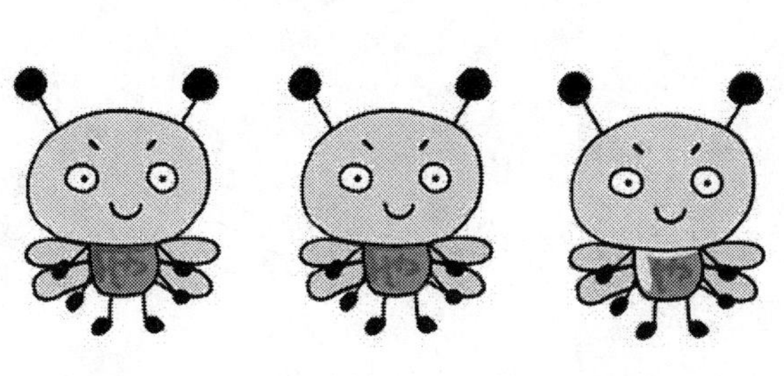

Something happened! The three brothers mutated into "Super Motivated Bugs." Normally when sprayed with CCPM gas, most bugs become "Motivated Bugs." But in this case, since they had already studied lots of CCPM, they mutated into Super Motivated Bugs.

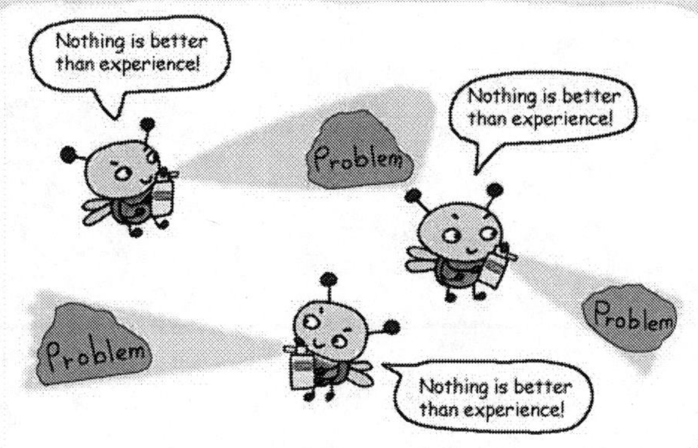

CCPM is very easy and effective. The more they studied and practiced, the more they came to understand the deeper logic. They had a lot of fun!
When people encountered problems, they came to spray CCPM gas on the them immediately, proclaiming, of course, "Nothing is better than experience!"

They then became known as the three Super Motivated Bug Brothers, and became more and more popular everywhere. Because of the good job these brothers did, the village prospered forever more.

Happy, happy ending!

Part 5 Sharing a Common Goal

目標共有

Session 01 Sharing a Common Goal

The Goal of the Project

In order to manage the project successfully, the most important key is to start correctly from the beginning. In other words, it is extremely important to share a common goal; "Well begun is half done."

Most project problems are caused by issues related to vaguely conceived goals that are not shared among project members. Sometimes a due date is fixed but you don't know what the goals are yet. Sometimes the goal is simply stated as "to develop the best product in the world." That mind-set is great, and should be appreciated, but the project members sometimes get lost in such a vague goal, rather than getting motivated.

The market changes, and your organization may change at any time. So sometimes it is not worthwhile to bother with the future too much, rather you might think it is better to concentrate on what you can do today. You think, "One step forward might bring you a more extensive view". In the meantime, it is not uncommon for the goal of the project to change repeatedly, spoiling project members' motivation and causing progress delay or even project failure.

ODSC (Objective, Deliverable, Success Criteria) to Share the Goal

Excellent project managers always stress the importance of SURIAWASE in developing a project goal. SURIAWASE[47] is a Japanese word that means to "come to a consensus." Project managers take time and work intensively to fine-tune the goal among all project stakeholders before starting. They think it is very valuable, and indispensable for the project's success. Everybody knows the importance of SURIAWASE, but in the past it has been considered to be very difficult—something that can be practiced only by experienced project managers. However, there is a very simple but powerful solution that enables everyone to do this just as easily as they do.

47. ODSC was developed by Ms. Deirdre (Dee) P. Jacob, managing partner of Avraham Y. Goldratt Institute, LLP. When I met her I expressed sincere appreciation to her. What I was surprised by was that she liked the word SURIAWASE very much.

The solution is to breakdown the goal into three categories: Objectives, Deliverables and Success Criteria. This is called ODSC. Using this solution, let's make an ODSC for the vague goal of "developing the best product in the world," as mentioned before.

ODSC

What are the objectives for developing the best product in the world? This is discussed among project members, and it is highly recommended to involve all people associated with the project, including senior management.

What is the purpose of developing the best product in the world? It may be to realize unprecedented profit, to beat competitors, to increase the market share, to make customers happy with breakthrough performance, or to make a great first step toward a world-class brand. When successful, it will foster personal growth for project members because they will be recognized as a great development team, having made a remarkable product. If it is the best product in the world, it will definitely contribute corporate social responsibility. It may help all project members learn how to reduce product development lead time, while reducing overtime work, enhancing teamwork across the organization, and keeping a discussion going so that all members are excited about the objectives. They are:

-Realize unprecedented profit.
-Beat competitors to gain the lion's share of the market.
-Make customers happy with breakthrough product performance.
-Make a great first step toward a world-class brand.
-Provide opportunities for member's personal and professional growth.
-Learn project management to reduce product development lead time while reducing overtime work and enhancing teamwork across the organization.

There are a variety of people with a variety of roles and responsibilities within the organization. Each person has, in fact, a different background and role, and everybody's interest in the project will be different accordingly. The discussion of the Objectives helps to reveal and pickup on the variety of unique interests that exist in the organization. Sales have their own unique interest, as well as project members, senior management, etc. During the discussion of the Objectives, it is recommended to discuss them as openly and freely as possible, so that all stakeholders, as well as project members, can put their opinions out to be shared. It is recommended to check six perspectives: the financial perspective; the customer perspective; the process perspective; the employee perspective;[48] the corporate philosophy perspective, and the corporate social responsibil-

48. The first four perspectives are proposed as part of the *Balanced Scorecard* by Robert S. Kaplan and David P. Norton, a financial perspective along with customer, process, and employee perspectives.

ity perspective. Everybody knows the importance of stakeholder support to the project's success. By checking these six perspectives, you make sure to get the necessary support from all stakeholders. It is always quite interesting to see senior management's reaction if the objectives clearly incorporate the company's philosophy and motivate senior management to support project success. Everybody knows the importance of the corporate philosophy, but it is not easy to educate all employees so they practice it as a regular exercise in their daily activities. This is why companies put posters of the corporate philosophy on the wall, to make sure employees understand it and to remind them to practice it as a day–to-day business exercise. But making this a reality is very difficult, as everyone knows. However, by seeing a project objective clearly reflecting corporate philosophy, it makes senior management happy, and they are willing to extend their help to make the project successful. Also, by doing it this way it helps to indoctrinate both the corporate philosophy and a sense of corporate social responsibility into project members naturally, without special attention.

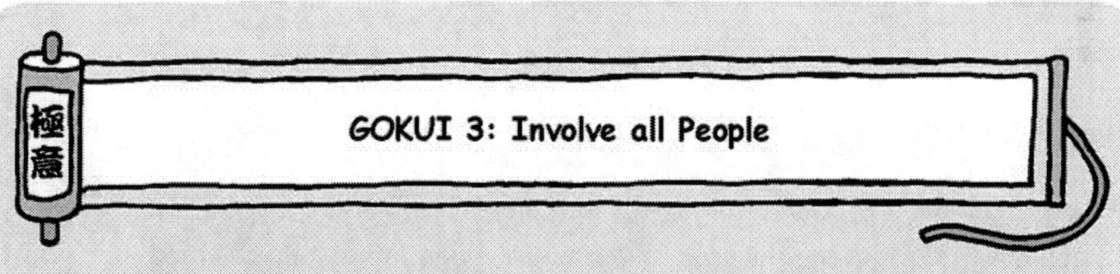

It is commonly said that the beginning is important. Therefore the SURIAWASE discussion becomes indispensable to the success the project. Involving people as much as possible, including all project members, leaders, managers, and senior management will help to gather various explicit and implicit knowledge from throughout the organization. Two heads are better than one, and three are much better than two. The more you get the attendees into the discussion, the better the ODSC will be. In fact, many times I have experienced hundreds of people gathered in the same room discussing the goal of one project, and cheerful discussions were radiating! You can't imagine how much energy I feel everyday in such atmospheres all over Japan.

Deliverables

What do you need to produce in order to achieve the objectives discussed above? Is it a product only? No. You need a manual, packaging, a brochure, a project network proven to reduce lead time drastically and, of course, people who associate project management with personal growth:

-Product X
-Manuals
-Package
-Brochure

-Increased share and profit
-Project network which can be reused, with modification, for the next project
-Members who understand project management to practice and train other people
-Quality time with family

In many cases, our biggest problems are caused by confusing deliverables with objectives. As you can see, these deliverables are designed to bring the objectives into reality. In other words, they are the necessary conditions—the *means* to make the project successful. However, in traditional project management, the deliverables get more attention since they are something to be *produced* by the project. This situation becomes worse if you are in trouble as the due date approaches, since your focus is much more attuned to making products, at all costs, by the due date. Thus, the mechanism exists to confuse the means with the objectives. However, if you conduct an ODSC discussion, the means are clearly differentiated from the objectives, and project members' minds will be more focused on the objectives, instead of the means.

Success Criteria

The previous two discussions showcase the objectives and deliverables among all project members. Now, in the Success Criteria discussion, it must be clarified, one point at a time, what the criteria are for success in this project. In this discussion the success criteria are:

-Product release by the date XXXXX, 3 months earlier than the competitors
-Unprecedented profit of 40%
-Superior product performance by 50%
-Within the top 10 by the next brand recognition research report
-Market share exceeds 50%, sales $XX millions
-Environmental product performance 10% CO_2 gas reduction
-Reduce quality problems to half of that of the current product
-Win XXXXX award from the industry society
-Reduce overtime work by half, with zero work over weekends
-Allow the CEO to say, "I am very proud of this team and have decided to make this a best practice of this company."

The Success Criteria must be something you can evaluate. You may find it difficult to establish success criteria that can be quantitatively evaluated. However, if it is expressed like the above statement—*Allow the CEO to say "I am very proud of this team and have decided to make this practice company policy, extending to all departments"*—it will be easily understood. In fact, in most cases, when this type of expression is incorporated into the Success Criteria, it stimulates everybody's brain to visualize what will happen if the project is successful, and we find it is very effective.[49] Please note that each of the Success Criteria listed here is a sufficient condition to declare this project remarkably successful.

Read Aloud

When finishing this dialogue, please read it aloud in front of all project members. If you see all project members smiling cheerfully, with motivated faces, the ODSC is completed!

These things are not new to you at all. May I remind you of what you would do previously when faced with serious problems in a project? You wouldn't discuss them among project members only, but you would also involve stakeholders, as well as senior management, and the first thing you would discuss was the goal of the project. It is natural, a matter of common sense, when you face a serious problem. The only new proposal here is to do this in the beginning.

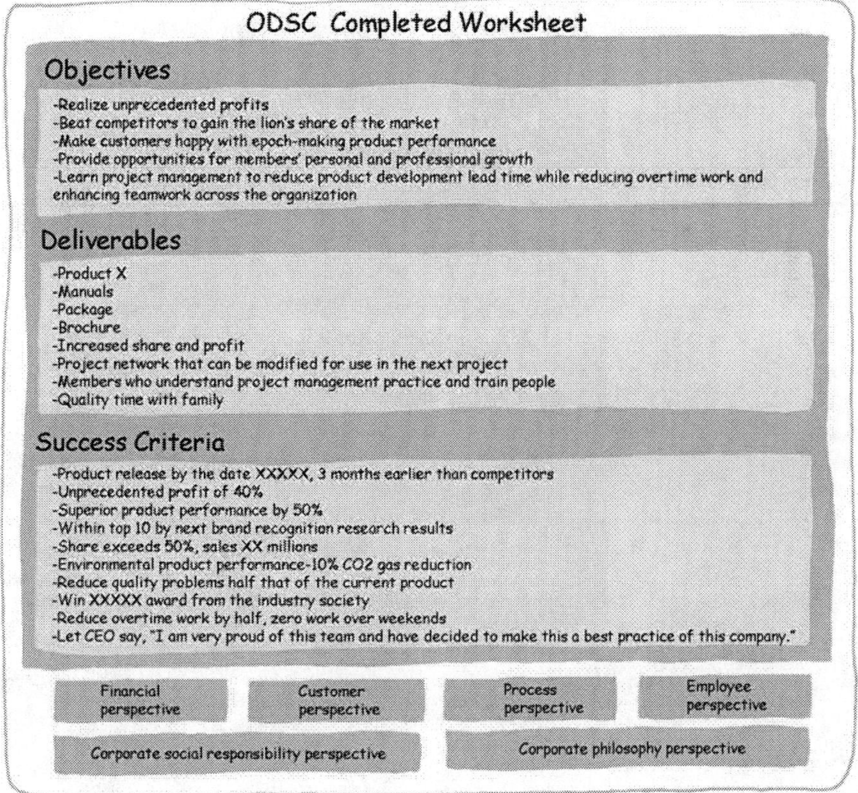

ODSC Completed Worksheet
Objectives
-Realize unprecedented profits
-Beat competitors to gain the lion's share of the market
-Make customers happy with epoch-making product performance
-Provide opportunities for members' personal and professional growth
-Learn project management to reduce product development lead time while reducing overtime work and enhancing teamwork across the organization
Deliverables
-Product X
-Manuals
-Package
-Brochure
-Increased share and profit
-Project network that can be modified for use in the next project
-Members who understand project management practice and train people
-Quality time with family
Success Criteria
-Product release by the date XXXXX, 3 months earlier than competitors
-Unprecedented profit of 40%
-Superior product performance by 50%
-Within top 10 by next brand recognition research results
-Share exceeds 50%, sales XX millions
-Environmental product performance-10% CO2 gas reduction
-Reduce quality problems half that of the current product
-Win XXXXX award from the industry society
-Reduce overtime work by half, zero work over weekends
-Let CEO say, "I am very proud of this team and have decided to make this a best practice of this company."
Financial perspective
Customer perspective
Process perspective
Employee perspective
Corporate social responsibility perspective
Corporate philosophy perspective

49. A friend of mine, a medical doctor specializing in the human brain, once told me that it is really effective to turn on the switch in the brain to focus on the project's success.

Well Begun is Half Done

If you would like to practice a famous cliché of project management, "Well begun is half done," it is highly recommended to have an ODSC discussion to share the common goal in the beginning, rather than trying to fight fires after facing serious problems (which consumes lots of time and money). If you would like to avoid fighting fires, you should spend thirty minutes discussing the ODSC, doing SURIAWASE on the project goal, and sharing the common goal among all project stakeholders.

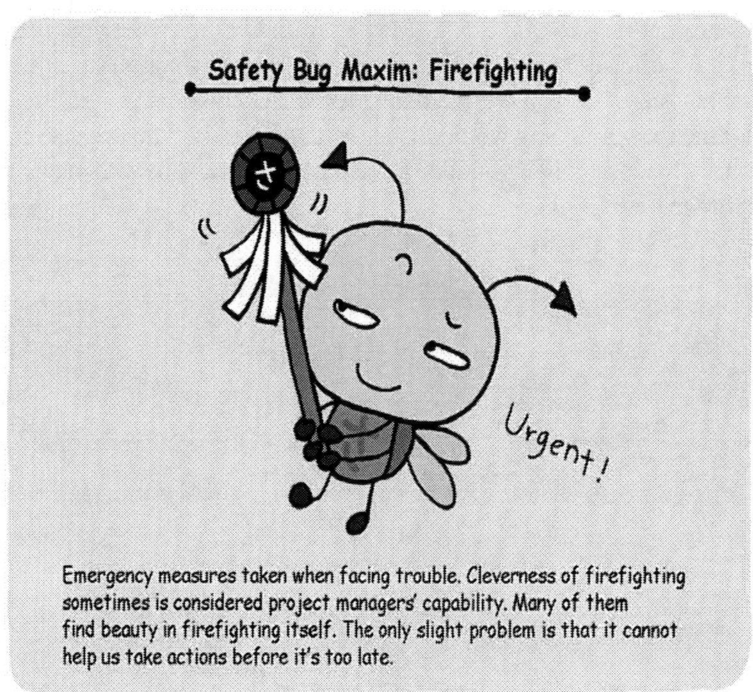

Safety Bug Maxim: Firefighting
Urgent!
Emergency measures taken when facing trouble. Cleverness of firefighting sometimes is considered project managers' capability. Many of them find beauty in firefighting itself. The only slight problem is that it cannot help us take actions before it's too late.

GOKUI 4: Put Words of the Soul into the Success Criteria

It is people who execute a project. Sometimes earthy, soulful words can be very powerful in motivating project members. If you see statements like, "Allow the CEO to say 'I am very proud of this team,'" incorporated into the success criteria, it accelerates project teamwork, and increases the chance of project success dramatically.

My favorite example is one from a consumer goods development project. They had a hard time with a popular big convenience store chain that had never handled their products before. During the Success Criteria discussion, they listed the following words: Let Y-san, senior purchasing manager, say, "By all means, please let us handle your new products." It really marshaled and energized them to lead the project successfully, because they could visualize a practical scene where Y-san begs to handle their new product.

Projects always encounter uncertainty. When facing it, project members tend to focus on producing the deliverables, sometimes losing focus on the project goal. But, as in the above case, they can be reminded by saying, Can we still see Y-san begging, "By all means, please let us handle your products"? It is a powerful reminder to all of the members to focus on the project goal, rather than the deliverables. The deliverables are the means of the project, not the project goal itself.

Earthy, soulful words will echo repeatedly among the project members, leading them to stay focused on the success criteria throughout the project, and will be very powerful and effective tools for driving project success.

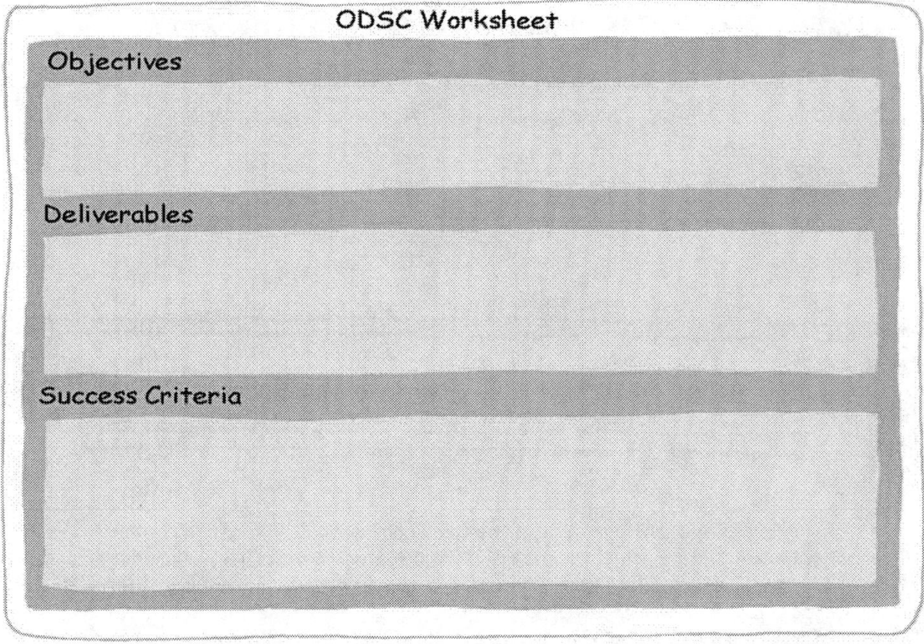

ODSC is TAIGIMEIBUN for the project

It is commonly recommended to make TAIGIMEIBUN (a common cause) for the project. The ODSC is the breakdown of TAIGIMEIBUN (which consists of the objectives, the deliverables, and the success criteria to be shared among all project members), accelerating teamwork and achieving project success. In order to establish TAIGIMEIBUN by using ODSC, I always check the following:

-Does it have the six perspectives: financial; customer; process; employee; corporate philosophy, and corporate social responsibility?
-Does it meet management's policy and project goal?
-Does it encourage all members' motivation with "aggressive but possible" goal setting?
-Does it meet the morals of the society? (Make sure to incorporate a societal contribution perspective.)

These are great lessons that I have learned from many excellent managers all over Japan. I personally feel the most important point to check is the aspect of societal morals. Recently, there have been many scandals that have raised the concern of morals in corporate activities. Since the majority of companies' activities are intended to make money, and management performance is thus evaluated, people tend to do inward communication to make this happen. Putting too much focus on making money can cause people to sometimes stop paying attention to the morals of society. To achieve severe management targets, they sometimes incorporate risky contents into the ODSC. This is very dangerous. All companies and organizations belong to society. It is very important to check whether their activities are outside the morals of the society, as it can damage the brand severely and might put people's livelihoods in jeopardy.

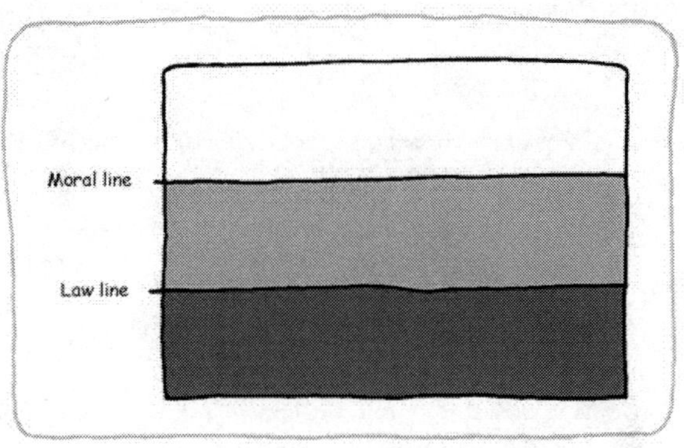

However, there is a very good way to avoid this, which is to make sure to incorporate a societal contribution perspective, as is most often listed in the corporate philosophy, into the ODSC. This will stimulate project members' motivation, and enhance support even outside of the project members. I did not know why until recently, but now I have come to understand the reason. Please take a look at this chart. In society there might be two lines: one is the law line and the other is the moral line. Activities that fall under the law line people call criminal. Activities that fall between the law line and moral line people call immoral—they do not violate the law, but they don't gain respect in society either. Activities that place above the moral line people naturally respect, because they have moral value. Most corporate philosophies have various statements in line with society's morals. When these statements are incorporated into the ODSC, it accelerates WA within the society, thus you naturally gain more support, even from people apart from project members who have nothing to do with your project.

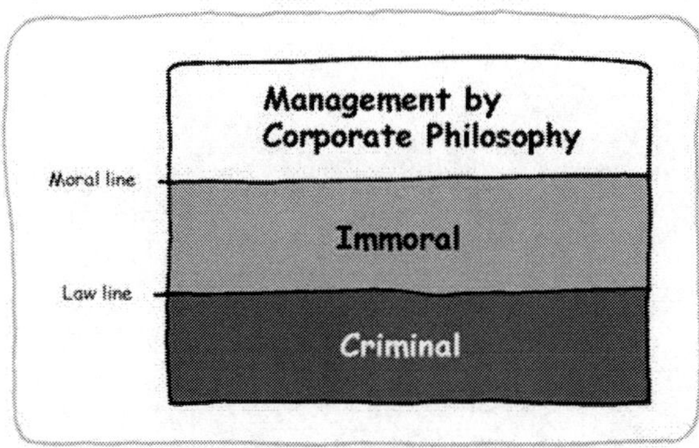

Again, this is not new at all. Omi merchantmen are very famous throughout Japan as successful businesspersons. In Omi business there is SANPOUYOSHI (win-win-win), one of the most important and cherished business principles from years and years of experience. It means: good for customers, good for us and good for society.

GOKUI 5: Set Goals Higher to Make the Project Successful

There are always discussions about how much more aggressively goals can be set.
Our experience teaches us an important lesson—the higher the project goals are, the greater the project succeeds.
A project's goals should essentially be linked with corporate management goals. With the six perspectives of financial, customer, process, employee, corporate philosophy and corporate social responsibility incorporated in the ODSC, it naturally encourages support from senior management, other organizations and suppliers. However, if you set goals that are easily achievable, other people will sense that you are manipulating the safety and are discouraged from supporting your project's success. With low goals it is difficult to obtain support from outside the projects, while high goals accelerate other people's support, and could even increase the opportunity to obtain support from an authority in the industry who is impressed by, and shares in, your lofty goals.

Session 02 Personal and Professional Growth with ODSC

People Grow During the Project

During the discussion of ODSC, I always strongly recommend that you put in your personal growth perspective.[50] For this particular project experience it is important to put in how you want to grow, what you would to like to be after project completion, how members want to grow, etc.

I have participated in a variety of projects where I have seen remarkable growth in the project members and felt my own growth, too. When looking back at these moments and seeing this remarkable growth, it was always when the success of the project overlapped with the members' personal growth. It is the time when a sense of mission is born, and the success of the project overlaps with member's personal growth, that the chance for project success is dramatically increased.

As repeatedly mentioned, it is people who do the project. It goes without saying that members' morals and passions play important roles in the project's success. Thus, it is natural that people emphasize the importance of TAIGIMEIBUN and a sense of mission. To incorporate project members' personal growth into the ODSC increases the chance of project success and drives personal growth. It is a "killing two birds with one stone" solution.

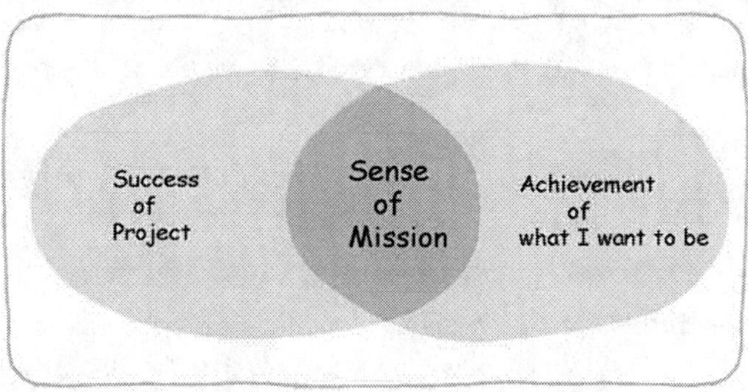

50. Projects by nature bring you to encounter things that you have never experienced. So, they are naturally related to personal and professional growth.

Why is TOC the Theory of Constraints?

I have faced situations many times where I have been asked questions like, "What is the difference between Toyota Projection System and TOC?" or "What is different about TOC? It's only common sense that has nothing new for us."

Now I have come to understand that such discussions make no sense.

According to the Oxford dictionary, a theory is a formal set of ideas that are intended to explain why things happen or exist. What Dr. Goldratt has been trying hard to do is not to develop new systems, but to develop a "theory" that can explain many management methods universally, in a united form, with simple logic. This is why it is called a theory, not just a set of systems or methods. It is sometimes called common sense, but does it matter? I don't think so.

When people see an apple falling from the tree, its path is considered natural, or "common sense." When Isaac Newton saw it, he saw the theory of gravity. When Dr. Goldratt sees common sense, he sees a theory of constraints in it.

In his book, The Goal, he states in the introduction:

"Science for me, and for the vast majority of respectable scientists, is not about the secrets of nature or even about truths. Science is simply the method we use to try and postulate a minimum set of assumptions that can explain, through a straightforward logical derivation, the existence of many phenomena of nature."

In fact, TOC is a very convenient tool to logically analyze and explain the best practices on Japanese shop fl oors, so that everybody can understand and practice them easily. On top of that, it is very simple. As we practice TOC, we see beauty in its simplicity, and this sometimes reminds me of the beauty of the Japanese culture of WA, such as a Japanese garden, Japanese painting, etc.

"Knowledge should be pursued, I believe, to make our world better-to make life more fulfilling."

-Dr. Goldratt, from the Introduction to The Goal.

I quite agree with his idea. As he is making his knowledge public domain, I want do the same to make all of our lives more fulfilling, and hope this book brings some of hints for making your life more fulfilling.

Part 6 DANDORI HACHIBU

段取り八分

Session 01   DANDORI HACHIBU

With a common goal discussed and shared in the ODSC, the next step is to make a plan for how the ODSC can be successfully realized. There is a very simple and easy, but powerful, way to do it, which is DANDORI HACHIBU planning.

Catch the 10 o'clock Train

Suppose you are in the office and you want to catch the 10 o'clock train. What would your thinking process be in order to achieve it?

"In order to catch the 10 o'clock train, I must buy the ticket by 9:55. In order to buy the ticket by 9:55, it will be better to leave here at 9:40. In order to leave hear here at 9:40, I must get this job done by 9:30. Okay, to confirm this, I will complete this job by 9:30, then leave here at 9:40, then buy the ticket by 9:55, then I can take the train at 10 o'clock."

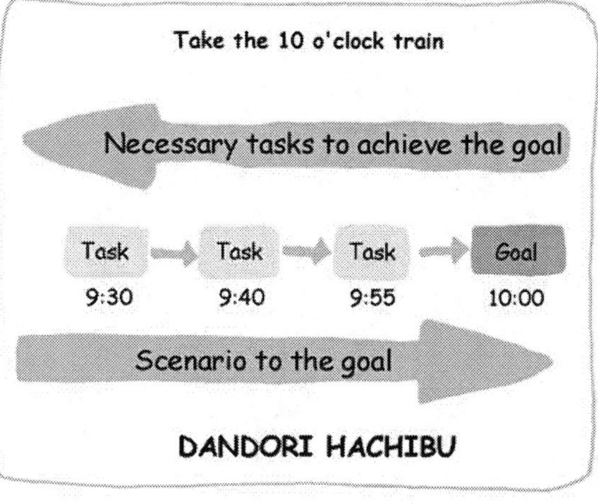

This is a very natural way of thinking for people. They will think in a backward manner when planning, and think in a forward manner when make sure those plans things happen. It is common sense, a natural way for people to think. At project management sites all over Japan, there isn't anyone who doesn't know "DANDORI HACHIBU" as the most frequently used and appreciated words. The literal translation of DANDORI HACHIBU is that "the preparatory plan is 80% of the project's success." However, it is a mystery how everybody knows that this is true, but nobody knows how to practice it. It has been regarded as a feat only experienced managers can accomplish, achieved by intuition and polished through accumulated experience. However, when I introduced backward planning, they agreed that this is the way they think.

Make DANDORI HACHIU Plan

To make a DANDORI HACHIBU plan is very easy, just ask the following questions:

"What tasks must be completed immediately before this task can be started?"
"Are there any other tasks that must first be completed?"

Simply continue asking the above two questions, staring from the final task and working backwards, until you reach the very first task of the project. When you have this dialogue, you will realize this team discussion is very effective for ensuring completion of all the planned tasks necessary to achieve the goal in the ODSC. Realizing this is the real essence of DANDORI HACHIBU. This is a good opportunity for you to discover what other persons are doing in terms of preparation and procedures regarding all of the tasks in the project.

You may notice that these two questions are designed to create a logic network, using necessity-logic and sufficiency-logic; you are now creating a network to *logically* achieve the goal discussed in the ODSC.

Present Tense Verb + Noun

It is important to write each task in a "present tense verb – noun" structure. By doing it this way, people naturally consider the task duration and the real task description to be shared with all of the project members. But, it is more than that also. It is much *easier* to understand in this way. Expressing tasks in a "present tense verb – noun" structure makes people discuss in them ordinary terms, rather than using complicated technical words or jargon, which sometimes confuse and mystify other people.[51] If other people don't understand the tasks as well as you, you cannot expect their support. **If you would like to have other people's support, you had better express all tasks clearly, so that other people can understand them.**

---

51. Why do people use complex, difficult words? It seems it's just to confuse and mystify others. Since these words are vague, most people do not understand their real meaning, and this can enable the manipulation of safety. Most of the people who use these words carry big responsibility, which means they need more safety than ordinary people like us.

During the discussion among all project members, it is effective to include experienced people's knowledge and senior management's advice, which can then be absorbed into DANDORI HACHIBU project plans as explicit knowledge in the task network. In general, most excellent project leaders are good at communicating complex and difficult ideas in an easy and understandable manner so they can obtain other people's support. It is ordinary people who do the tasks in the most cases, so it is natural to express tasks in a way that ordinary people can understand.

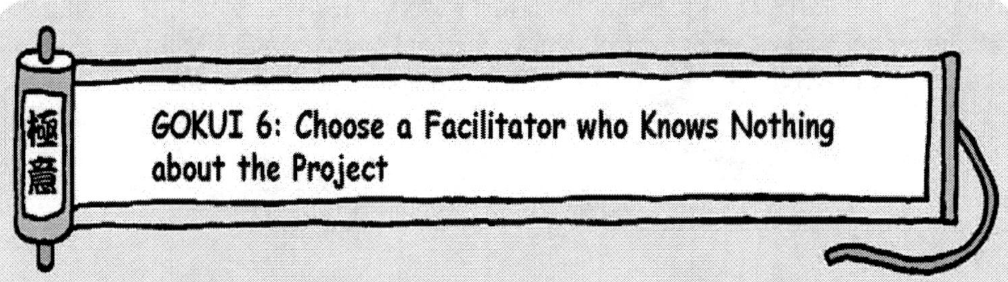

極意
GOKUI 6: Choose a Facilitator who Knows Nothing about the Project

Traditionally, the facilitator must be an experienced person who has skills such as coaching technique, etc. However, my hundreds of experiences let me believe this is not a requirement. In fact, it is recommended to ask a person who knows nothing about the project, a green person, such as the youngest person on the project, to facilitate. When he or she plays the role of facilitator, the discussion is tailored so that he or she can understand, as if experienced project members are teaching him or her. This helps to transfer the knowledge of experienced persons to a younger generation.

Please don't worry if he or she brings up the wrong task or procedure. These wrong tasks and procedures stimulate experienced people to give them valuable advice (I don't know why, but I was advised that it was because it reminded them of their mistakes earlier in their career).

Do not ask an experienced person to be a facilitator. When this is the case, project members come to the discussion looking to the experienced people, and sometimes people are afraid to speak up. The discussion then gradually turns into persuasion from the boss to the members, where common goals are hardly discussed and shared.

Anyway, it is easy to practice it. By simply asking several well designed questions, an inexperienced person can play the role of facilitator easily, and it is even a good opportunity for providing on-the-job-training. I personally love to be a facilitator on a project that I know nothing about. It is a great opportunity to learn many things, and sometimes I feel as if I use other smart people's brains to make a network that in no way could I generate alone. Think and let think. In fact, it is especially fun because I feel I am really participating in the projects even though I don't know anything about them.

Forward Check

Once you have completed the backward planning, the next step is to read the tasks in a forward manner. You will find it very easy to read since all the tasks are written as present tense verb-noun, with each task dependent on another, just like the scenario for project success. Read each task aloud, one by one, to confirm the task contents and the interdependencies that lead to the goal. This is a stairway to achieve the project goal discussed in the ODSC. [52] If there are any missing tasks discovered by way of this discussion, just add them in to make the plan better.

Simply read aloud the tasks in the following manner:

"If you do A, then you can do B, correct?"

Reading these tasks is just like telling a story of the project's success, and you will see all of the members' faces smiling and full of motivation, convinced that the goal are achievable through everybody's teamwork. I have done hundreds of projects in this manner, in various kinds of industries, and I am always amazed that just a few hours of discussion can really create such a high quality task network (which had often never been made before) with exciting, "aggressive but possible" goal

You may notice here that you are checking this with cause and effect logic, making sure all tasks and interdependencies *logically* achieve the goal discussed in the ODSC.

High Risk Tasks Pushed Earlier

When having this dialogue, you will notice that the tasks associated with high risk are naturally pushed earlier in the timeline. Because the network is constructed in a backward manner, using necessity-logic, high-risk tasks are necessarily pushed toward the beginning. Until now, experienced people have started with the high risk tasks, while inexperienced people have started with the tasks they think they can handle themselves, often resulting in later revisions, and proving the lessons: "More haste, less speed" or "He who begins many things, finishes but few."

However, when the project tasks are discussed among team members and involve experienced people, the experienced people will provide valuable advice, such as "Do A task (high risk task) before B task (lower risk task)." The mechanics of both tasks remain the same, only their interdependency is different. This sequence will disclose potential risks

52. I am a vocalist specializing in singing LED ZEPPELIN songs. My voice is so close to Robert Plant's that sometimes people think I might be haunted by Robert. Sorry, he is still alive. *Communication Breakdown* is my favorite song. Sometimes, it's strange to me that my job is to cure the communication breakdown in organizations.

much earlier, or could eliminate potential problems in the future, since it reduces the risks dramatically. This way, people learn a lot from experienced people about DANDORI HACHIBU. It also follows the rule of project management discipline—to do high-risk tasks upfront. It is a very effective way to systematically train inexperienced people in the planning stage, and to teach things that used to be learned only through experience.

On-going KAIZEN in the Estimation

There is a mix of tasks within a project. There are the tasks that you can estimate with relative accuracy, and there are others you cannot. There are always tasks with high levels of uncertainty, which you cannot know until you really start them.

These are the tasks that need to be started earlier in the project duration, so that the uncertainty can be identified and the risk can be estimated. This means that the uncertainty will be dissolved in the initial stage, and your estimation will become more accurate as the project advances. This naturally increases the chances of keeping the due date. It also helps to develop forward thinking skills for project members, which is very important for the project's success.

Making a Scenario for Project Success

Here the resources and estimated durations are filled out for the project tasks. It is recommended to fill them out in a forward manner, just like making a scenario for a story of success. Who is going to do it, and for how long, will be filled out for each task, just like casting the actors for an individual scene (called tasks) in a success story.

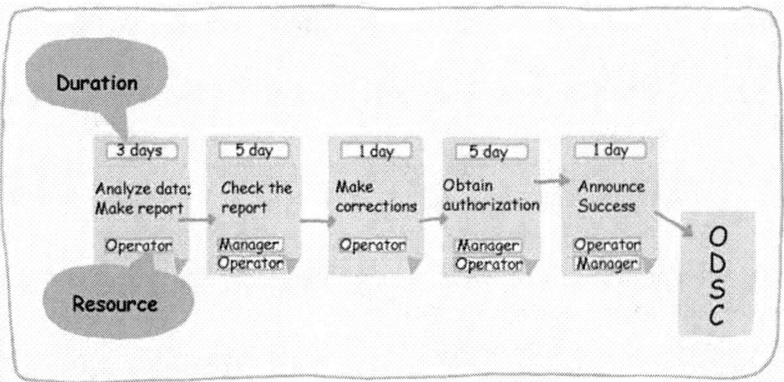

Projects have become more and more complicated recently, involving many organizations, where sometimes the projects are carried out with a vague sense of responsibility for who does what. Sometimes it causes the situation where everybody assumes other people will do certain tasks, and it ends up that nobody does some of them, causing serious problems in the project. So, this process of discussing who does what, and for how long, is extremely important.

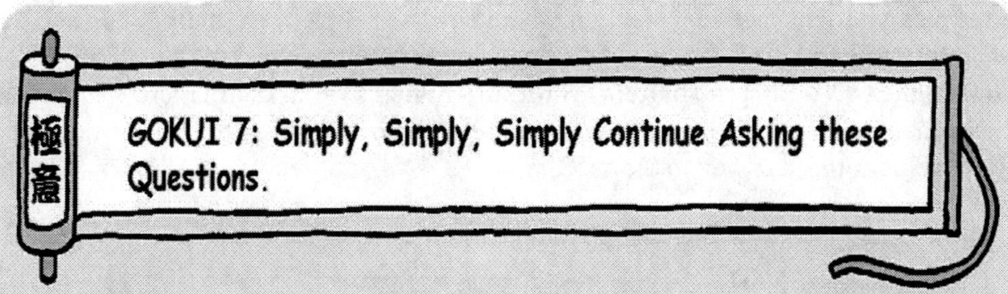

極意
GOKUI 7: Simply, Simply, Simply Continue Asking these Questions.

"What tasks must be completed immediately before this task can be started?"
"Are there any other tasks that must first be completed?"
"If you do A, then you can do B, correct?"

These three questions are carefully designed to make sure you achieve the goal through necessity-logic, sufficiency-logic and cause-and-effect logic respectively. It is very important to check with all project members to see if the network can logically achieve the goals. If everybody agrees with it, it will really be a roadmap of the logical steps to achieve the goals. While the goals are very aggressive, all members are convinced that there is a logical way to succeed (with the buffer being the source of teamwork), and their motivation will be increased.
According to David C. McClelland, an American personality and social psychologist, people are highly motivated by:

1. A situation where success is dependent upon a person's own efforts and ability (not luck).
2. A situation where the challenge or risk level is medium (where your subjective chance of the success and failure is 50/50 percent).
3. A situation where there will be clear feedback as to whether you have achieved the goals or not after all of your efforts.
4. A situation that requires innovative solutions.
5. A situation that requires you to make a plan by forecasting the future in forward looking manner.

Do these sound like similar to CCPM? In fact, most of the people who are practicing it feel this way indeed.

If you discuss this within your project, you will realize that the assignment of resources is extremely important. Depending on who does the task, the duration will be significantly different. It may take a long time if you only assign engineers, but with the involvement of a senior manager, it may help to reduce task duration dramatically. But there is more to it than that. The discussion may disclose a situation where one engineer is being exploited for a variety of tasks, and alternative resources would be beneficial. Sometimes you will face the situation where several people raise their hands and say, "We'll take this task," since everybody shares a common goal and responsibilities from knowing the ODSC and the buffers. Since the contents of tasks are more clear, senior management can easily understand what they have to do to make the project successful. This concludes the stairway to the success.

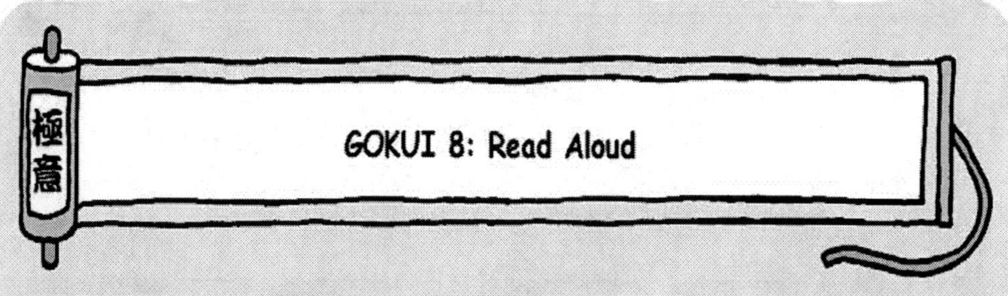

It is very important to read aloud when you check all tasks in a forward manner. For the previous scenario, it can be read:

If...
"the operator analyzes the data and makes a report in 3 days,"
then...
"the manager and the operator check the report in one day"
If...
"manager and operator check the report in one day,"
then...
"the operator can revise the report in one day"
If...
"the operator revises the report in one day,"
then...
"the manager and the operator can get approval of the report in one day"
If...
"the manager and the operator get approval of the report in one day,"
then...
"the manager and the operator can make a presentation of success"
...and achieve the ODSC of the project goal

By reading aloud, all members can visualize the success story. Also, by checking the scenario and achieving ODSC, it further motivates all of the team members; it convinces them that if they follow the scenario, it will lead them to success.

Session 02 Share the Safety

Due Date First

The longest chain of tasks is the constraint of project duration that you can focus on to reduce the duration, with a holistic view in mind.

However, our reality is usually, "The due date is set before the beginning of the project," and you find it almost impossible to meet. It is in very rare cases that you can quote the time and tasks accurately enough to set a realistic a due date or budget. But our reality is that we most often are told, "The due date is this!" and "The budget is this!" The tougher the competition is, and the more important the project is, the more likely the due date and the budget will be fixed for some unknown political reason. Thus, when managing projects, you generally need to meet a fixed due date (or earlier) and budget (or less).

Don't Remove Safety, but Create YUTORI to Share

In general, there are three major methods to remove safety. One is to snip it. Since there is always safety in a task due to people's sense of responsibility, to just snip the task duration in half is one of the possible ways to remove the safety from the task. However, it is more difficult in a practical sense. Imagine if you were forced to do this, you would not be so happy about it.[53] Another method is by communication. By discussing each task, you can review whether the estimated duration is really 50/50, "aggressive but possible." You just keep on asking, "Is it 50/50?" for each task, while providing some advice for how to reduce the task duration.[54] This is a good and effective way to do it, but you may find it tedious at times. The most recommended method is by creating YUTORI through team discussion.

---

53. Once you experience this, you will add twice as much safety in the future since you know your boss will snip it in half. It is human nature.

54. "Is it 50/50?" is "Goju Goju Desuka?" in Japanese. Dave and Rodger who taught us CCPM used this phrase in Japanese during our initial CCPM course. Everyone found it interesting and started to use these words (with an English accent!) when taking the safety out of their tasks. It's now becoming a buzzword in many companies in Japan. (Dave and Roger are consultants from Afinitus Group in North America. https://www.afinitus.com/)

Steps for YUTORI Creation

Step 1: Create a task network, working backwards. Then set the duration as the team would like it – *you don't have to discuss the 50/50 duration, rather encourage all members to enter the duration which they feel has adequate safety.*

Step 2: Convert the task network into a Gantt chart.

Step 3: Create the project buffer by identifying the critical chain and calculating 50% of the critical chain duration, and place the buffer in the project network. Do the same for the feeding chains. Then, check to see if the ending date of the project meets the real due date for the project. Normally, we hear, "Oops! It doesn't meet the due date!" That is only natural, because each task already has safety included, and the buffers are then added in on top of that.

Step 4: Check the long tasks on the critical chain.

Step 5: Discuss how to reduce the duration of these tasks, one by one, beginning with the longest. (It is recommended you conduct this discussion in the task network, rather than the Gantt chart). An effective way to reduce the duration is not just to reduce the duration of each task one by one, but instead to break down the tasks, combine the tasks, review the tasks which can potentially be done simultaneously, and to review the task sequences. The task network gives you a simple, birds-eye view, so you can intuitively understand the entire picture and holistically discuss, among all of the team members, how to effectively reduce duration.

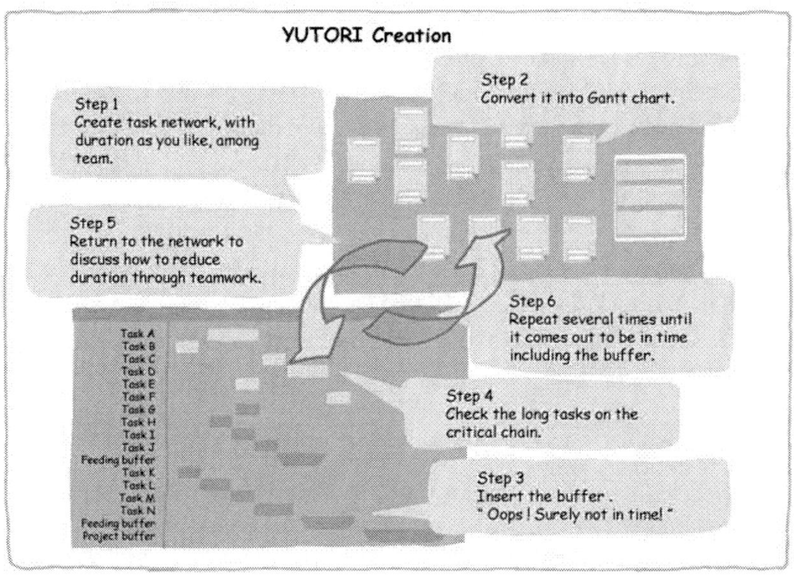

Repeat Steps 2 through 5 until you meet the due date, including whatever buffer size you want. With a common goal, as outlined in the ODSC, shared throughout the discussion, you will find it much easier to obtain other people's support (senior management's in particular). While it may seem rather exhausting to discuss each task one by one in order to remove the safety, you will find it enjoyable to discuss YUTORI creation because it will stimulate team discussion. You may start to see everyone working very intensively, exchanging ideas as one big cohesive team. Since uncertainty is the nature of projects, everybody wants to have as much buffer as possible. In order to keep the buffer as big as possible, everybody intensively discusses all tasks on the critical chain, and **you find the discussion now transforming from how to remove the safety in the task, to how to create YUTORI through teamwork.**[55] By creating a sense of cohesive teamwork, and obtaining all kinds of support from other departments and senior management, project members feel motivated, with spreading trust and harmony—WA throughout the company. In fact, during the process of YUTORI creation, you will feel as though you are going back and forth between now and the future, and everybody is convinced that it will happen simply by following this plan as a team effort. It is very powerful since you really feel you can change your future!

In fact, I have seen numerous projects that were in jeopardy emerge with a bright future by going through the YUTORI creation process. I hope you will try it in finding the beauty of WA.

Several Practical Considerations to Reduce Duration

Although people can understand the need to remove safety from each task, due to their sense of responsibility, they still want safety as much as possible. In order to exploit the constraint, each task on the critical chain needs to be checked, one by one, to see if there is any hidden safety. An effective way to do this is to verify each task, beginning with the longest.

Let me introduce several ways to do it:

Reduce the task duration itself

First, discuss why the task duration is so long. Team members will find it very easy to understand the tasks and their sequence, since each task is written in a present tense verb + noun sentence, a common form of expression that allows other people to understand the story easily (and possibly offer some help). Read aloud to make sure each task is necessary to do the next task(s). People are people, and safety is always important with a sense of responsibility. However, people sometimes tend to overdo tasks, trying to perfect elements that are not essential. Make sure everyone understands that shared safety will be added back as a buffer, serving to protect

55. It is just a discussion of whether to remove safety or to create safety. Both are essentially the same but creating safety sounds much more positive.

everyone. The safety in each task will also be shared among project members and will become a source of teamwork.

You may find some tasks take far longer than others. These are often tasks that are associated with other departments or organizations. Since they are believed to be out of the control of the project members, they tend to estimate large amounts of safety for them. Although project members work very hard on their own aggressively estimated tasks, the majority of the duration on the critical chain often comes from safety added to the tasks of other organizations. This is where you need to get them involved in this discussion. By knowing they are eating the majority of the duration, even as project members are working with their own aggressive durations, intensively discuss how to help this situation succeed. Also, it will not be difficult to involve them, because the project tasks are written in a way that is easy to understand. And again, it is a good idea to involve senior management, since the goal written in the ODSC are so good that senior management will be naturally motivated to support you.[56]

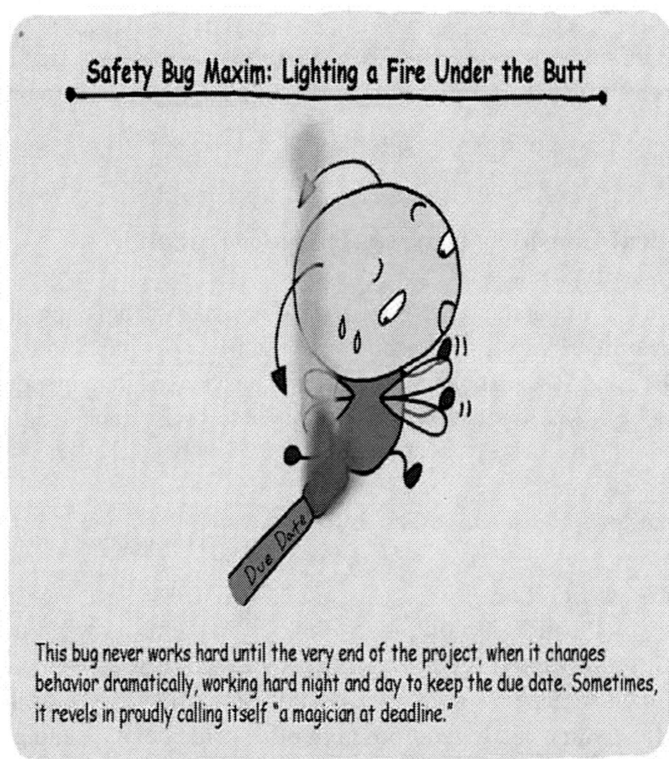

Safety Bug Maxim: Lighting a Fire Under the Butt
Due Date
This bug never works hard until the very end of the project, when it changes behavior dramatically, working hard night and day to keep the due date. Sometimes, it revels in proudly calling itself "a magician at deadline."

56. I once hated to hear the complaint "We need more time and money!" from project members. However, now I am voluntarily involved in helping them, and since the project goals written in ODSC are so attractive to me, I cannot help but support them. In fact, now project members come to me saying, "We can really achieve this aggressive goal only if you do this." This phase really motivates me to support them a lot, since now I know clearly what I should do to make this project successful.

Break down the task

It is a good idea to break down the long tasks into several smaller tasks. Uncertainty is the nature of projects. The longer the task, the more the uncertainty increases. By breaking down the task, you can make a more accurate estimation, or prepare much better DANDORI. By breaking down a longer task, the duration is reduced in several ways. When there are smaller tasks, often several can be done simultaneously. Some portions of the task can be prepared beforehand, and advance notice to the other organizations can accelerate their support. These are things to be discussed among the team members, and to be reflected in the task network.

Combine the tasks

It is also sometimes a good idea to combine two or more tasks into one. Multi-tasking is not good, but there might be some tasks that can be effectively combined, creating a synergy effect. This is not multi-tasking. Practically speaking, it should have been one task originally, but it was divided into several tasks due to historical reasons, organizational reasons, or just standard exercises born of some unknown reasons. You need to check to see if these tasks can be effectively combined.

Review the task sequence

It is a good idea to review the task sequence on the critical chain to see if you can reduce duration. It may be quite surprising, but this is much more effective than just concentrating on each task individually. During the discussion to review the task sequence, members will come to understand how an erroneous sequence might lead to later revisions, causing a longer duration. This is the great lesson; the sequence of the tasks, in other words, DANDORI, is extremely important. The beauty of DANDORI HACHIBE is recognized by practicing it.

A project is a chain of tasks that you have never done before. This dialogue helps to exchange ideas, strategies and tactics among the project members so that they feel more comfortable in executing the tasks with good DANDORI. It may be better to think of this dialogue as a basic part of the project's design, rather than project planning work.

How many times have you heard the importance of teamwork stressed during a project? If everybody knows the importance of the project, then you had better plan projects through teamwork, not through the project leader alone.

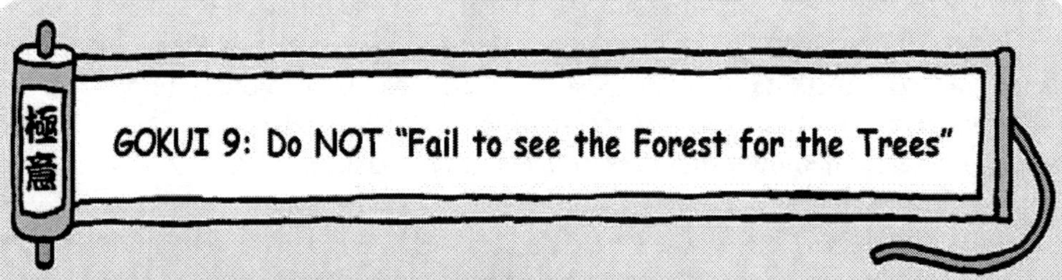

極意
GOKUI 9: Do NOT "Fail to see the Forest for the Trees"

What is the appropriate task size? What is the appropriate number of tasks? It is very important to view the project from a holistic standpoint when you want to make sure everything is right. It is a good idea to go back to the purpose of project management here. If the purpose of project management is to meet the project goal through a team effort, with high quality results, then the answers will be obvious:

-In order to obtain support from other project members and senior management, you need to state each task so that it is easily understandable to others.
-In order to exchange ideas for better DANDORI among team members, you need to make the tasks as large as possible, ensuring the tasks on the critical chain involve everybody for the YUTORI creation discussion.
-In order to keep a holistic view in mind among the team, you need to reduce the number of tasks as small as possible.
-In order to make sure everybody does a good quality job on each task, you need to avoid multi-tasking.

People are people. Do you expect a good job to be done if you are doing different things every hour? How about every half hour? How about every 15 minutes? It is quite obvious that the quality of the job will decline. What do you call it if you are doing different tasks every 15 minutes? Is it called "multi-tasking"?
Sometimes, people want to make sure they don't miss a single detail. This is good and right. But every detail is not listed in the project network, because a checklist is sufficient for that. In fact, when you discuss YUTORI creation, you will naturally discuss the task duration at the level of people's assignments, so they can discuss the job effectively and reduce task duration. It is common sense that it is people who do the project. And if you remember this, it is common sense that you should set the task duration at the size of people's assignments, so they can effectively and efficiently work at doing a quality job.

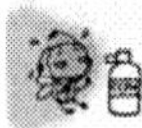

Innovation R&D Needs Iterations

In research and development activities, it is indispensable to conduct trial and error iterations. The DANDORI HACHIBU discussion is a very effective and practical method for this.

A project is always accompanied by limited time. If you discuss the project goal with the ODSC, it should clearly have the due date that you must meet to succeed with the project, and it becomes very obvious to everybody that unlimited reiterations of trial and error are not allowed. A project, by definition, has limited duration, with a limited amount of trial and error, before it hits the due date. When you create the project network with the numbers of iterations required, it will make clear the number of iterations allowed.

For example, this chart shows the early stage of a new development project that needs trial and error iterations. Conducting an experiment requires at least a 20-day duration, with the verification of the results over an additional 10 days. Suppose the company needs to make a project plan that must be completed in 120 days. 20 days planning and two iterations of the experiment will already take 80 days, and in a case where three iterations are necessary, you will need an additional 30 days to conduct an additional experiment (20 days) and review the results (10 days). This means 80 days + 30 days = 110 days. However, there is great amount of uncertainty in the research, so there needs to be a buffer of at least 50%, which is half of 110 days = 55 days. If you add 55 days to the 110 days task duration, it will be 165 days. This is already is beyond the due date of 120 days from now, and requires you to reconsider the plan. In order to keep the buffer of 50%, while keeping a due date of 120 days, project members will realize that they must complete it in two iterations, a plan that consume 80 days + 40 days buffer.

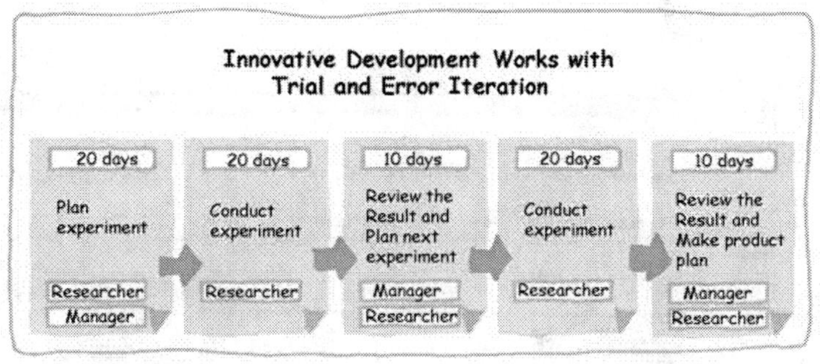

It is actually good to share the common understanding that everybody must work very hard to complete experiments, with the spirit of a challenge (of only two iterations), and the 40 days buffer will allow them to conduct one more iteration, just in case. In the execution stage, the initial iteration will probably be prepared far more precisely, since everybody knows the initial iteration is the key to completing it with just two, and the second iteration will be fine tuning, to confirm the miscellaneous things that will make a good product plan. Notice that the iterations are no longer just the repeat of the same experiment but each iteration has an individual meaning or purpose. However, even with a good preparatory plan, you may fall in to a situation where two iterations are not enough, and you will need a third (for which you have the buffer). Of course, the third trial might fail sometimes also. But even in this situation, you may find the buffer consumed is only a portion of the whole project buffer, which consists of not only the two iterations, but also of the subsequent tasks which have far less uncertainty associated than the early stage of research and development. You will find there is still much more time to recover from the delay, far before it becomes too late. Since there is a common goal in the ODSC, shared with senior management and other associated organizations, it enhances support for one another, building a strong tie between researchers and senior management, fostering strong competitiveness in the marketplace.[57]

You will definitely find this is the most practical way to run innovative research and development activities, because only CCPM has an innate buffer to protect from the uncertainty in the project. The more uncertainty increases, the more effective is the buffer. It is common sense. So, the more uncertainty you expect in your project, the more effective CCPM will be.

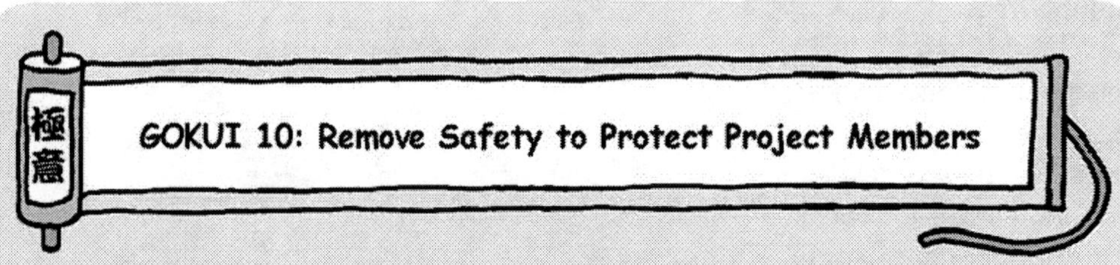

極意
GOKUI 10: Remove Safety to Protect Project Members

With CCPM, senior management understands the "aggressive but possible" challenge duration of the tasks, and that project members are doing them without safety. They also know the importance of the project as written in the ODSC. Thus, they will hesitate, or at least think deeply, before assigning additional tasks, since they know it will directly impact buffer consumption. Removing the safety from each task eventually protects all project members from an increasing scope, while providing a good working environment to focus on tasks without interruption.

You may be afraid that with CCPM the project has little flexibility in terms of potential changes or additional requests. This is absolutely NOT the case! In fact, there will be more logical flexibility. Remember there is the buffer, which helps you decide whether you can comply with changes or additional requests from a holistic management point of view.

57. In fact, CCPM implementations for research and development are the most active in Japan, especially in markets having really tough competition and short product life cycles. One senior manager said to me, "There is nothing more important than managing new product development, since it is *management itself.* If you develop the product or technology much earlier than your competitors, you can sell the product at a higher price, and increase market share and profit. This leads to a higher share price, strengthening the financial base of the company and enhancing long term competitiveness. There is nothing more important than this."

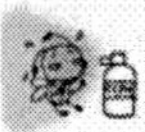

Concerns/Risks During the Project

It is very important to discuss the potential concerns and risks during the project. A good question to ask is:

"What problems, if any, do you anticipate in completing this task?"

By asking this question, concerns and risks are listed, followed by an exchange of ideas on how to avoid them. This allows countermeasure actions to be incorporated as tasks in the project network. There may be some actions that project members cannot handle, since they are associated with so many high-level management issues. These tasks should be listed as requests to management.[58]

The Real Meaning of the DANDORI HACHIBU Project Plan

Please review the project plan once again. Throughout this discussion, project members have acquired a shared will to achieve the goal by listing only necessary tasks, with the least potential for missing tasks. This is because now all members have been involved with identifying the risks, as well as the countermeasures and requests to management that are intended to avoid them. To make things better, everybody associated with the project confirms with each other that they will use teamwork to achieve the common goal described in the ODSC.

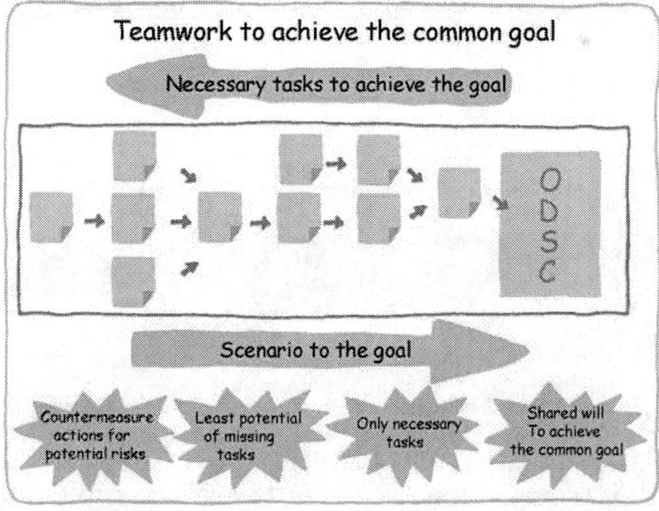

58. In my experience, it is more effective to incorporate a rewards-type list of requests to management, which motivates project members to achieve the ODSC completely. If the goal described in the ODSC is high enough to motivate senior management, the requests will be accepted easily. By using this method, I have seen many projects exceed the success criteria in the ODSC, allowing companies to give paid vacation, bonuses, etc. In a sense, the high goal sometimes plays the role of the carrot for both project members and senior management.

The DANDORI HACHIBU Project Plan will be a Valuable Company Asset

The project plan generated through the DANDORI HACHIBU discussion is now a valuable company asset, containing all the knowledge of the company, gathered through a collaborative effort. By reviewing it, you will easily understand how you can re-use some portions in other projects. It visualizes all of the implicit knowledge existing throughout the organization, allowing you to manage projects better. In other words, this DANDORI HACHIBU project plan is your winning formula, a standard that will evolve each time it is re-used.

Company Assets Evolve

The most common comment from companies that have implemented CCPM is, "The one thing that pleases us the most is the personal growth of project members." It goes without saying that the most valuable asset in the company is its *people*.[59] Since it is people who do the projects in corporate and organizational activities, the importance of people is becoming more and more significant. As has been discussed frequently, implementing CCPM will eventually develop human resources, since CCPM focuses on people management.[60] Spreading trust and motivation throughout the organization, while transferring implicit knowledge developed by years of experience to younger generations via well-designed communication, supports personal growth and enhances the most valuable asset of a company, *people.*[61] This may be the most dramatic effect of CCPM.

59. Companies, which are developed by humans, are sometimes referred to as having personalities. However, financial statements, which are supposed to disclose the personality of the company, reveal little about people. Speaking in the extreme, if all employees are removed from a company, the company ceases activity. I reviewed several technical books on financial statements, and every book stressed the importance of people. This convinced me to focus on people. It is more fun anyway.

60. Professor Ohara of Nihon Institute of Technology, who is famous as the developer of P2M (Project & Program Management for Enterprise Innovation) a Japanese standard for project management, calls CCPM "human-centric project management."

61. One of my friends, an industrial medical doctor, said to me, "Your book is a prescription for mental health." So far it seems like he is right, since many people have more fun and are happier while motivated. Someday, I want to conduct scientific research on it.

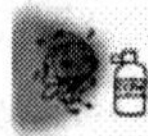

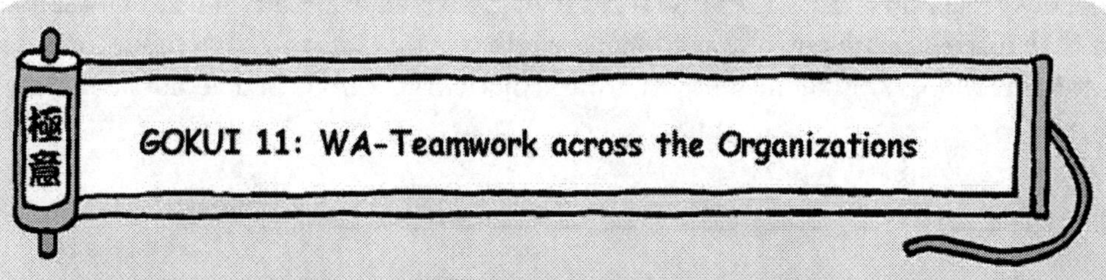

What you doing through DANDORI HACHIBU project planning is creating WA-Teamwork across the organizations. The majority of project members are not lazy at all, in fact they work very hard. To achieve project success, they will even stay up all night. The discussion of YUTORI creation, focusing on the critical chain, gives birth to an atmosphere where everybody works together to achieve the project goal as a team. The tasks with the longest duration are generally not the tasks done only by project members, but are the tasks that require involvement from other organizations, such as "get approval from customers," "procure tools from suppliers," etc. This is where project members naturally recognize that support from outside is indispensable, and senior management understands what they need to do to accelerate teamwork across the organizations. By practicing CCPM, trust is spread across the organization. I have implemented CCPM in hundreds of projects, and it is most commonly described as "fun" and "happy." I think this is because people feel fun and happiness when people work in a place where there is teamwork, trust, and harmony. This is called "WA."

Does my offer work?

Please take another look at the problems I discussed previously:

-The budget, resources, and time allotted to projects are often not enough.
-Decision making by clients or management is slow.
-Information is not shared in a timely manner.
-Delivery from suppliers is delayed.
-Scope evolves and increases often.
-Support is not obtained from management or other project stakeholders in a timely manner.

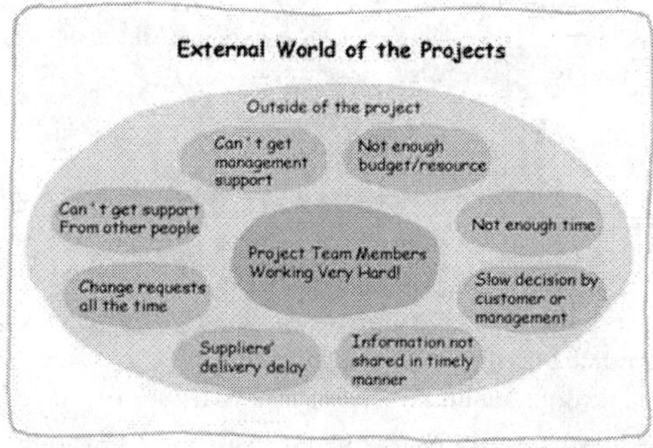

I hope you feel now that CCPM is worth trying. We have already noted that the ideas we have discussed are not new at all, but are rather common sense. Everyone must have heard something similar in the past from experienced senior people advising others, such as:

You had better:

-Make sure to share a common goal among all members.
-Exchange ideas and involve all people in discussing how to achieve success.
-Make sure to have a good preparatory plan, with only the necessary tasks and without waste.
-Enjoy the spirit of challenge.
-Help each other through teamwork, with safety in hand, just in case.
-Take action before it's too late.
-Advance the project with a strong sense of shared responsibility among all members.

These are not new at all; they are only common sense. CCPM just makes them possible as common *practice.*[62]

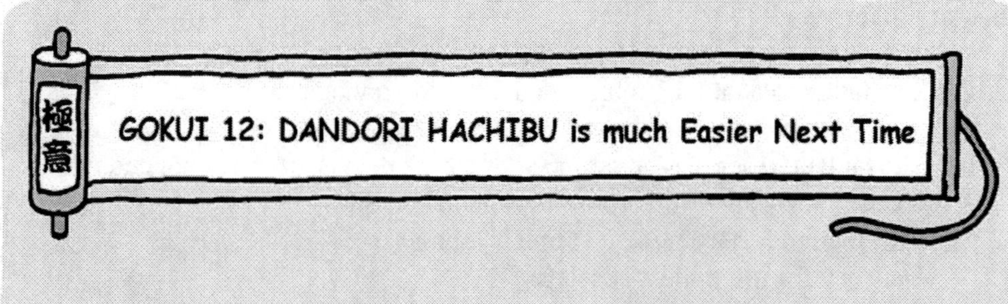

極意
GOKUI 12: DANDORI HACHIBU is much Easier Next Time

It may take time to do DANDORI HACHIBU at first, but it is rewarding. You may realize that you can re-use most of it in the next project. There are several unique processes in each company, developed over time and through experience, that are said to be the best practices of the company. They will be repeatedly practiced, and polished for better use, and will eventually become the ever-evolving standard of "know-how" in managing projects to success.

62. As I learned more and more about CCPM, I came to wonder why it was not the standard for project management, since it was so much common sense. But I didn't have to worry anymore when I realized that common sense has developed throughout human history by years of years of experience by human beings. It is natural to follow common sense if you want projects to succeed.

Session 03 Everyday is KAIKAKU with excitement

Continuous KAIZEN

Of course projects will be exposed to changes, that is their nature. In the worst cases, the project may fail regardless of everybody's efforts. Just make sure to learn a lesson from it. Failure is the origin of success. It provides a good opportunity for on-going KAIZEN if you ask:

"What were you waiting for?"

Then you will understand the problems better, and can discuss how to deal with them next time in YWT[63] format. YWT means:

Y: Yatta koto – what you did

W: Wakatta koto – what you learned

T: Tsuginiyasu koto – what you do next

It is quite simple and easy, but it is really very powerful as a learning exercise. KAIZEN, as a process, is on-going improvement that will incrementally increase the chance of project success as experience accumulates.

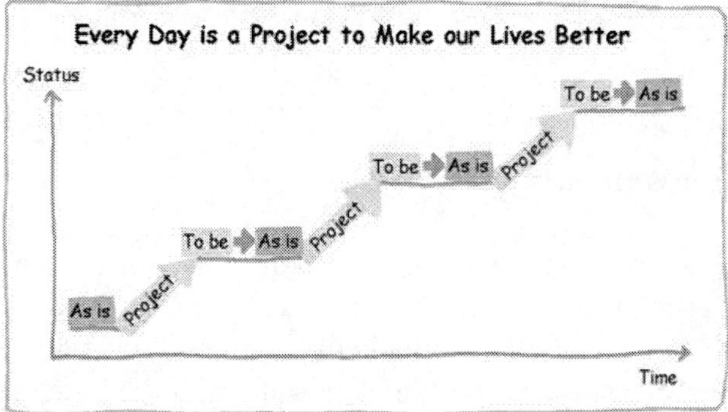

63. I learned YWT from JMA Consulting, Inc. in Japan. I like it a lot because it is very simple and easy yet powerful in practice. http://www.jmac.co.jp/e/

When a project succeeds, members will move on to their next projects with higher levels of confidence and trust, using enhanced teamwork to reach a common goal. Every day is a project, where we make our lives better and more fulfilling, motivated and supported by trust and harmony – WA throughout the organization.

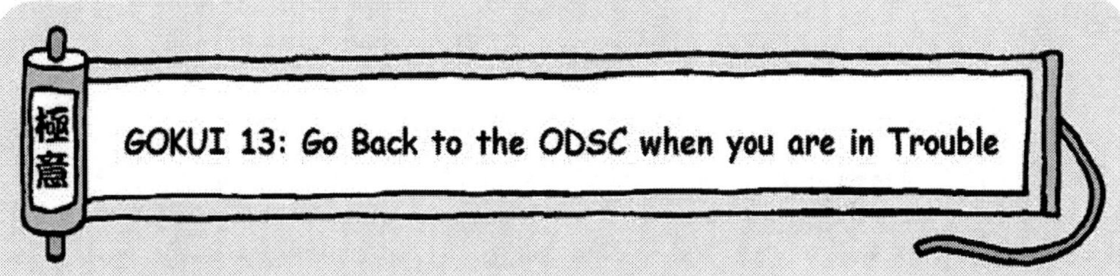

It is a very good idea to go back to the ODSC when discussing how to solve problems. People tend to focus too much on particular tasks during a project, sometimes losing sight of the overall goal. Going back to the ODSC gives project members a fresh reminder, and aids breakthroughs, even in difficult projects. In fact, the comments I hear from many excellent and experienced project managers show that it is quite a common and natural procedure to return to the original goals of the project when faced with serious problems. They intuitively break down the goals of the project into objectives, in order to clearly define the purpose. Then the deliverables are broken down to clearly define what is necessary to produce, and the success criteria are broken down to clearly define the sufficient conditions for bringing the project to success. There is one more good way to use the ODSC. Whether you are working on a project or not, when you face problems in the organization, creating an ODSC can help solve them. This is because the SURIAWASE discussion helps to highlight common goals. There are many departments, and people within the departments, that have a variety of different individual responsibilities. This often causes a silo mechanism where everybody is working very hard, but for the best interests of each department, rather than the entire organization. In this situation, dependable leaders will define the common goals, and facilitate a breakthrough discussion involving all people. It only takes about 15 minutes to create the ODSC once you become used to it; "Heroes appear like the gale and leave like the gale." It might be one of the secrets of dependable leaders.

Single Projects or Multi-projects?

It is multiple projects, not single projects, which are a fact of life. In fact, the method we have been discussing is much more powerful when you implement it in multi-project environments. This Figure shows the simple illustration of what we have been discussing so far. The effect of a single project implementation is illustrated inside of the circle. To share the common goal, ODSC is made through a SURIAWASE discussion. Each task written here is very easy to understand so that everybody can help each other dur-

ing the project. Challenging, "aggressive but possible" task durations motivate project members to plan how to do the tasks, glean knowledge from experienced people, and focus on one task at a time, while enhancing quality of and reducing task duration. Each sequence of tasks is carefully studied through DANDORI HACHIBU in order to create the best preparatory plan. Buffers make it possible to do SENTE KANRI, by building teamwork and "show-the-belly" trust throughout the organization.

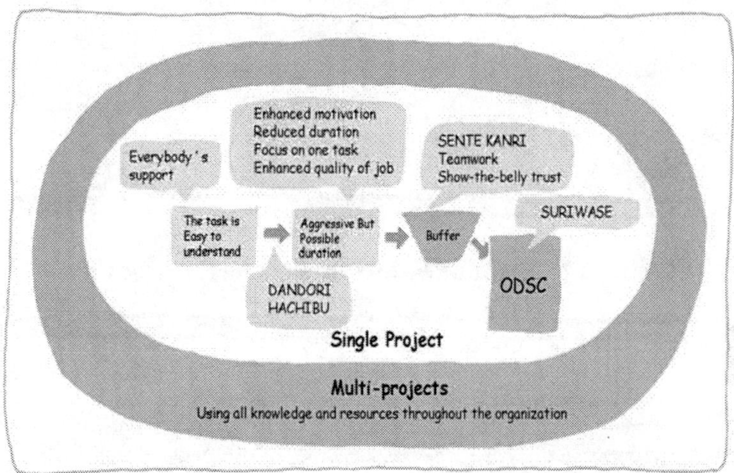

The effect on a multi-project environment is much more dramatic, since each project is enhanced by using knowledge and resources from across the organization. The SURIAWASE discussion is conducted to define the priorities of all of the projects based on a holistic view. Using all of the knowledge and resources provides greater flexibility in reducing durations, and drastically enhances the quality of tasks. It is natural that DANDORI will be much better by using all of the knowledge and resources of the organization. And the buffers shown across the organization make it possible to help each other between departments, with much greater flexibility, using all of the knowledge and resources. It goes without saying that the effect on multi-project environments is much greater than that on a single project.

This is not new for us at all. A sense of helping each other, and thinking things through by putting oneself in another person's shoes, is regarded as one of the most important virtues in Japan, where it has been practiced year after year as a moral of the society. It can be said that multiple-project CCPM implementation is a return to the origin of the Japanese culture of WA in management practices.

GOKUI 14: Use CCPM in the Toughest Situations.

It is always recommended to use CCPM in the toughest project situations. Since CCPM is planned by way of backward scheduling (with DANDORI HACHIBU), it is easy to apply it even in the middle of an endangered project. First, create the ODSC through a SURIAWASE discussion to make sure an exciting goal is commonly shared. This is then followed by the backward discussion, DANDORI HACHIBU, which will convince all project members to think, "Even in this difficult situation, it is possible to achieve such a goal. It is tough, but it can be done, since there is clearly a way to achieve it." Where there is a will, there is a way. The ODSC creates a will that is shared by project members, and DANDORI HACHIBU shows the way to achieve it. In fact, it is my observation that the tougher the situation is, the relatively easier and more effective it becomes to implement CCPM. It provides an atmosphere that makes teamwork much easier than in normal situations. Sometimes I see the effects of multiprojects, even in single project implementations; as the situation gets more serious, I am led to think that the unbelievable power created by the teamwork in the tough situation (like "the Incredible Hulk") might be the native strength of the organization. CCPM just makes it possible in practice.

Consensus and Making Judgments

Please, let me ask several questions.

First:

> "What are the two most important things for the company's continuous growth?"

Of course, they are employees and suppliers. Without support from employees and suppliers, you cannot expect the company's growth to continue.

The next questions are:

> "Do you practice cost reduction activities?"
> "What are the two most significant costs in your company?"

The most common answer will be the cost of employees and suppliers. It is quite interesting that these two are equally important and significant. Without big support from employees and suppliers, you cannot expect the company to grow continuously. It is common sense.

There were several decades when Japan showed continuous growth at unprecedented rates. When research was conducted by other countries, two significant differences in Japanese standard business practices were disclosed:

> -SHUSHINKOYOU (Lifetime employment)
> -KEIRETSU (A group of partner suppliers with sense of family)

People from other countries understood the beauty of the concepts above, and appreciated them very much. Regretfully, we have been gradually throwing them away. Regardless of the world's economic momentum, I still believe there is great hesitation in most Japanese minds.

It is well known that Dr. Goldratt would not allow his books to be translated into Japanese for almost two decades. I thought Dr. Goldratt did not like the Japanese, and when I met him in November of 2006, I boldly asked the question, "Do you hate the Japanese?" His answer was quite surprising to me. He said, "Absolutely not. In fact, I really respect the Japanese and Japanese culture very much. The three people I admire the most in Japan are Dr. Deming, father of Japanese quality activities, Dr. Taiichi Ohno, father of Toyota Production, and Akio Morita, co-founder of Sony."

One thing he admires the most is that Japanese culture values consensus. It is natural for Japanese to reach a consensus before making a decision. However, according to Dr. Goldratt, for other countries, it is common to make a decision first, and then garner consensus from others. It is sometimes called a bottom-up and top-down approach. By analyzing Japanese culture, he has come to understand that the Japanese have a consensus-first approach, which is so deeply rooted it's like it's embedded at the cultural system level.

Japan: Consensus → Make decision
Others: Make decision → Consensus

Ever since I heard his comment, I have repeatedly asked the same questions to hundreds of audience members at locations all over Japan, and I have come to believe he is right. I think that we Japanese feel a large amount of discomfort if the management takes a "Make decision → Consensus" approach, while if management takes the "Consensus → Make decision" approach, it really motivates people.

In TOC, there is a predominance of logic supporting the idea that "Consensus → Make decision" is foundational. So the Japanese feel very natural and comfortable with TOC and are easily motivated by it. This is the reason why Dr. Goldratt would not allow his books to be translated into Japanese. He was afraid TOC might drive Japanese competitiveness even higher in the world market (creating a larger imbalance) by re-discovering the beauty of Japanese culture logically.[1]

In the research previously mentioned, there was one large criticism aimed at the Japanese. This was the fact of slow decision making, or a lack of leadership in the "Consensus → Make decision" approach.
We Japanese call it NEMAWASHI (consensus making before making decision), which may not sound good. However, Dr. Goldratt found the biggest advantage in it. It is very enlightening.

1. In worldwide national sales of The Goal, Japan is number one. So, it seems he was right indeed

Part 7 Management KAIKAKU by YUTORI

ゆとりの経営改革

Session 01 Critical chain—of the People, by the People, for the People

I am the type of person who can learn only by practicing. In this way, I have come to realize that the critical chain is really a chain of people's spirit of challenge and motivation, that is connected by shared responsibility and a strong sense of teamwork, and that the purpose of the chain is people's personal and professional growth, through well-designed communication management.

In fact, by practicing CCPM, everybody feels a dramatic acceleration of communication between all project members and stakeholders. CCPM also provides a desirable communication platform across all organizations, one that allows the project to be successful.

-The SURIAWASE discussion of the ODSC is a communication tool used to share the common goal among stakeholders.
-The DANDORI HACHIBU discussion is a communication tool used to share the *means* by which to achieve the goal through teamwork, while providing project members a training opportunity to "think."
-The YUTORI creation discussion is a communication tool for project members, through teamwork, to focus on the most critical part of the project.
-The buffer is a communication tool used to encourage project members to practice SENTE KANRI (take action before it is too late), employing a holistic view, and making the right decision for the entire company, with the harmonious teamwork of the WA spirit.

There is something to be said for using common sense to attain project success. However, to practice common sense is extremely difficult in the real world. CCPM defines how you can communicate better during each individual phase, so that the project will be successful as a whole. It is a simple but extremely powerful method of practicing common sense.

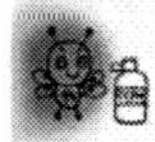

One more important thing to notice is that these communication tools will eventually develop trust throughout the organization, bringing more fun into the workplace. In the Japanese culture of WA, where collaborating and helping each other are regarded as virtues, CCPM is so natural that everybody accepts it easily, with little resistance. This figure shows a summary of the comments on CCPM, in regard to its increasing and decreasing effects. It is interesting to see that most of them feel CCPM is fun and amusing. Because it is people who do the project, this mentality is particularly important for dramatically increasing the chance of success.

Decreasing and Increasing by CCPM

Decreasing
-High pressure
-Negative discussions
-Waste of time and money
-Worry/Stress
-Accidents
-Complex documents and reports
-Conflict
-Silo decision-making
-Big enterprise disease
-Worry about resource development
-Irritation
-Complex discussions
-Errors/Re-work
-Overtime work

Increasing
-Flexibility
-Positive discussions
-Focus
-Safety
-Custom of thinking deeply
-Helping each other/Empathy
-Smiling faces/Happy employees
-Holistic decision-making
-Teamwork across organizations
-Wonderful personnel growth
-Fulfillment
-Profit
-Quality
-Time with family/Quality of life

極意
GOKUI 15: Communication! Communication! Communication!

Most people who practice CCPM will say, "It is amazing to get such an unbelievable profit in a such a short time. However, the best outcome of the project is people's growth." It is people who do the project, so it is only natural that with people's growth comes incremental increases in the chance of project success.
What do you do when faced with serious trouble during a project? You discuss it among team members, of course. In fact, most people do practice this in order to find a breakthrough, but with CCPM, this logic is embedded so deeply that it occurs far before the problems get too serious. The most important thing is communication.
-Exchange everyone's ideas
-Help each other
-Employ straight talk between the boss and project members

"Can I help?" "How about this idea?" "I have a suggestion to make it better." "How are you doing?" "Good job!" "Could you help me since I think it may become a big problem?" "Well done! Excellent!" "Thank you!"

Through these bits of communication, the project members will learn many lessons at the sites, and will grow both personally and professionally. It is really the best way for on-the-job training to lead to project success, where project members enjoy a sense of teamwork and fun in the workplace, and senior management can feel comfortable knowing they can take action far before the problems get too serious. The project members will have trust in senior management, and feel more motivated in their jobs. Senior management feels happy too, knowing all project members help each other, and that they can trust that the project management is dependable.
The most important aspect of project management is communication. Communication helps to establish a network of trust throughout the organization. CCPM accelerates this communication. CCPM motivates people, enhances their growth, and increases their commitment to the success of the project. In CCPM there is a systematic logic for building an environment of trust in which people can grow.

SESSION 02 Managing YUTORI

This figure shows the status of multiple projects. With buffers, the status of all projects across the company, regardless of the department, becomes clear at a glance. Furthermore, buffers are shown in simple colors (green, yellow and red), as indices for "a holistic view." Even top management, who are extremely busy, can grasp the situation easily and see where to focus their support. Any potential delays are reported long before it becomes too late, enabling specific "SENTE KANRI" actions. Projects advance and everyone, from management to the people in charge of tasks, make decisions, based on common criteria, from the perspective of holistic management and helping each other. This view shows a situation in which **"YUTORI" for all of the projects across the company is shared.** With the **"YUTORI" for the entire company** visualized, the focus of management shifts from managing the progress of each project individually, to managing "YUTORI" with a holistic view. With "YUTORI" in place, it is possible to *manage*. ***This is very important. "YUTORI" is "shared safety," gathered from the safety of each individual task, which originally was born from people's sense of responsibility.*** *In other words, the origin of "YUTORI" is in people's sense of responsibility.* ***Managing "YUTORI" means managing the sense of responsibility throughout the organization.***

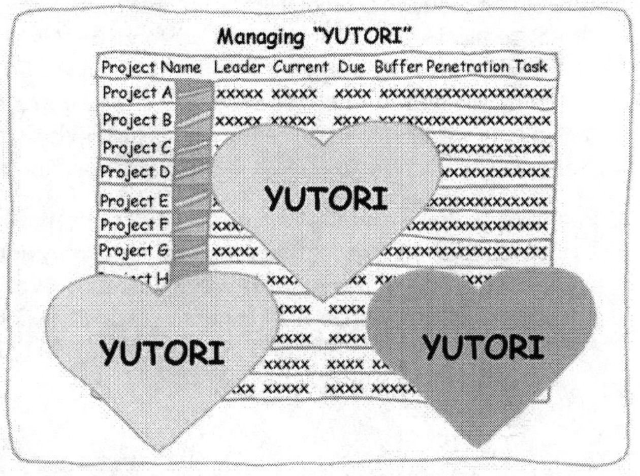

I have been involved in hundreds of CCPM implementations in various projects, including management transformation projects, software development projects, research and development projects, sales activities projects, etc. Within only a few months, project durations were shortened dramatically without increasing resources (even reducing outsourcing), and with dramatically better quality results. What is surprising to note is that the way meetings are run has significantly changed through exercising CCPM. Only the red and yellow projects are carefully discussed, focusing on forward-looking plans that can possibly help solve problems. Members of the green projects willingly offer help. Time spent on administrative project reporting is drastically reduced. Management participates from across the organization, and members begin to focus on discussions of "SENTE KANRI" as a team. Everybody feels increased "WA" throughout the organization. The workplace becomes cheerful and fun; some people start to say, "What's wrong if I am looking forward to Monday morning?"

Why does CCPM so Dramatically Reduce Durations?

When I implemented multi-project CCPM for the first time it was a great shock to me that, within just a few months, the lead time was dramatically reduced to roughly one fourth of what it used to be. There were a few hundred projects on-going, so it was really quite suprising that it was done without increasing resources, even while reducing out-sourced jobs, and with a drastic reduction to almost zero overtime work for project members.

For a long time I could not digest why it happened this way. Since then, I have continued to see the same things everywhere in Japan where CCPM is implemented. Now, through several years of experience, helping with hundreds of CCPM implementations in various kinds of industries, I have gradually come to understand why CCPM has such a dramatic impact.

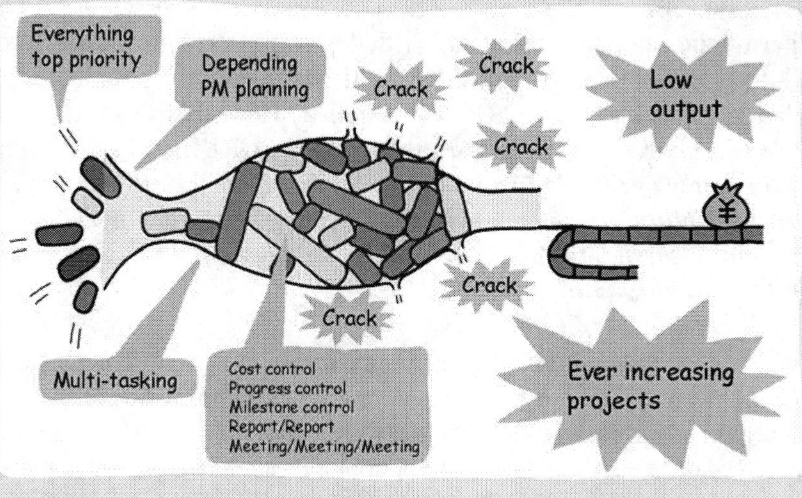

This figure shows a current project pipeline typical to most organizations prior to implementing CCPM. Everything is a top priority and all project plans are made independently by project managers. Multi-tasking is rampant, and there is intensive effort to control costs, progress, and milestones. This results in meeting after meeting, requiring excessive reports and paperwork. At the end of the pipeline, just before the product comes to market, requests for changes come from customers, sales, marketing and/or management. This increases the scope of the project, and slows down its completion. With an ever increasing number of tasks and projects, it causes very low output from the pipeline.[1]

This figure of a CCPM pipeline is much different from the previous one. Everybody has a shared goal, with a SURIAWASE discussion to create the ODSC. DANDORI is much better through the consensus of the team members. The YUTORI creation discussion enhances team members' motivation, while reducing lead time. Project members are allowed to focus on one task at a time, enhancing the quality of the job. Then, in the execution stage of the project, people will help each other by SENTE KANRI buffer management, with a spirit of teamwork. It is quite natural that this pipeline puts out more deliverables constantly and without pain.

1. Some people imagine this figure as a colon, but I don't intend it that way. However, now I have come to understand the meaning of the term "pain in the ass." I don't know why, but many people resort to "kicking ass" in such a tough situation. Do they know it only causes more pain?

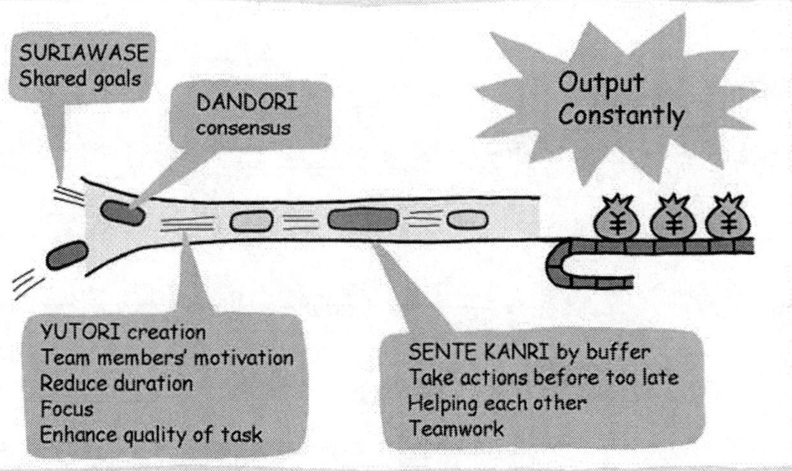

SESSION 03 Your Future Reality

I would like to talk about the figure that was previously discussed on page 11. How will it change if you implement CCPM?

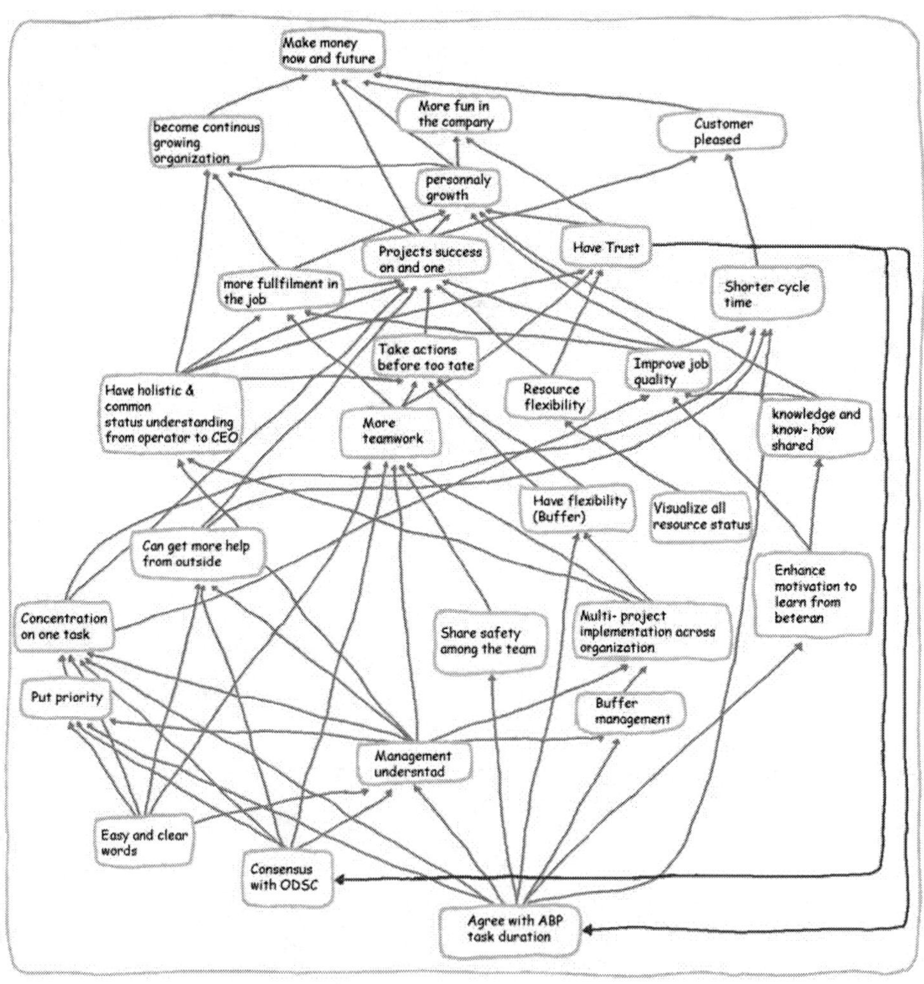

The cause and effect relationship discussed so far as a product of CCPM, is depicted in this figure as a visual summary. If project members are pursuing a high goal in the "SURIAWASE" discussion in the ODSC, and if they are consistently using aggressive but possible (ABP) durations for each task, then management will prioritize projects.

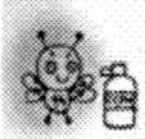

With priority and an "agressive but possible" duration for each task, project members can concentrate on one task at time. When members are challenging themselves with an "aggressive but possible" task duration, and sharing buffer with others, buffer management becomes possible. If buffer management is applied to multiple projects belonging to various organizations, flexibility for "SENTE KANRI" is enhanced, and action can be taken before it is too late. The "YUTORI" creation discussion is the best practice for the transfer of knowledge to project members. If the knowledege and expertise of experienced people are shared, and if project members can concentrate on one task at a time, the quality of work goes up.

With a "SURIAWASE" discussion in the ODSC, it becomes much easier to also obtain support from outside. If support from the outside is obtained by way of ODSC statements (which are created through a consensus of project members and stakeholders), and if buffer management is applied to multiple projects in the company, teamwork will accelerate throughout the organization and its associated stakeholders. If buffer management is applied to multiple projects in the company, everyone, including management, will have common criteria to determine which projects are a priority for rescue during the project process. This will drive people to take action before it is too late, and will result in more successful projects.

In an environment with teamwork, where high quality work is in place, project members feel motivated. People grow in such an environment, and the workplace becomes a happier and more cheerful place. If people focus on an "aggressive but possible" task duration, and engage in a high quality work with outside cooperation, then delivery time will be shortened. If delivery time is shortened and projects succeed one after another, clients are pleased. In an organization in which everyone has common criteria for decision making, and can work in an environment with teamwork, a sense of trust is fostered. If there is sense of trust in the organization, the project team can agree to a higher objective and will continuously challenge themselves with "aggressive but possible" durations. If members feel motivated to do their daily jobs, everyone works together in a spirit of teamwork, projects succeed one after another and the organization will grow. In a growing organization, if projects succeed one after another and clients are satisfied, and if people experience personal growth and the workplace becomes a happier and more cheerful place, then the organization will continue to generate profit.

The figure on the following page is overlapped with the figure from page 8. Nothing shown in the figure from page 8 is wrong. Experienced managers always talk about the importance of these items; they are exactly what experienced managers intuitively understand. However, when each item comes up from time to time in terms of a philosophical perspective, and is stressed to project members, they often become no more than vague mental exercises. How to achieve them is beyond understanding, especially to inexperienced members. By comparison, in the overlapping figure all items are logically connected. It is far more understandable and helps people make an effective and holistic management transformation.

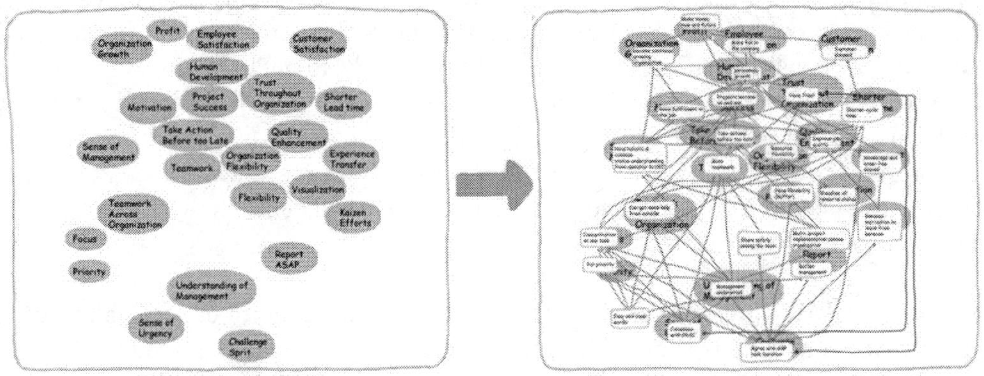

Figure from page 8

Figure from page 120 is overlapped

CCPM is not just Project Management anymore

TOC (The Theory of Constraints) is a theory for holistic transformation management. In providing management consulting services to the various project-oriented industries, TOC consultants have analyzed multi-project environments (ie. the construction industry, research laboratories, the software industry, the high technology industry, etc.), and are able to disclose the common problem that plagues them, namely that each and every person and team works very hard individually, but does not necessarily contribute to a holistic performance. These experiences resulted in the development of CCPM as a generic solution for holistic management transformation in project-oriented industries.

The reality of corporate activity is based on the multi-project environment, in which the ideas of CCPM were originally developed. The purpose of corporate projects is to achieve business goal. With CCPM, the business goal is clarified by defining the project using the ODSC process. Setting management priorities, in order to continuously achieve the business goal, and to "make money now and in the future," follows. It is natural for project deliverables to change even while the project is being executed. In these cases, it is the *business objectives* that should be focused on rather than the deliverables. With buffer management, we can take action before it becomes too late. Each task is eventually linked to the project goal, which are discussed and verified using cause-and-effect logic. Projects are managed in the real world, where we cannot guarantee 100% project success. A certain project might fail for unavoidable reasons. Even though this is the reality, with the holistic view necessitated by the corporate multi-project environment, it is possible to achieve the business objectives of the entire organization by making up for one failure with another project's success. CCPM was developed to manage projects by sharing buffers with a "holistic system view." In short, CCPM provides the logic of "Management," or *how to manage*, not individual projects, but multiple projects with the perspective of a holistic management view.

Excellent project managers in Japan always put emphasis on "people." This fact speaks the truth: *When one looks at tasks, it is neither the technology nor the machines that perform the execution. It is the "people" who carry out the tasks.* Managing "people" is decidedly important if you truly wish to manage projects.

It is said that TOC is based on common sense. As such, people often "take it for granted." However, in our real world, where multiple projects are complexly intertwined, and participating departments have interests which often conflict, there is nothing more difficult than to practice business based on common sense. CCPM, understanding this complicated reality, offers a simple but practical method that anyone can practice in order to manage multiple projects with a holistic management view—to yield the greatest output for the whole organization. Dr. Goldratt once pointed out that TOC is a methodology that is extremely suitable for the Japanese people, who respect harmony. Harmony is "WA" in Japanese. In Japan's first constitution, dated 604AD, the first charter starts with "Respect WA." It is not an exaggeration to say Japanese culture is deeply rooted in "WA." In fact, "WA" means harmony, peaceful, sum and Japanese. Indeed, many people in Japan have responded positively to CCPM, saying, "It is so natural to us." As the methodology of TOC itself is based on the philosophy of Win-Win, it is highly compatible with other methodologies. I have been practicing the implementation of TOC together with a variety of Japan's best practices, which seems to have a synergetic effect on accelerating the speed of success.

There is a Specific Medicine to Cure the Big Enterprise Disease!

According to the dictionary, the "Big Enterprise Disease" is defined as a name for evil human behavior generally present in big enterprises. This is characterized by a "vague presence of responsibility, lack of communication, slow decision making, lack of flexibility, disregard of the sites and lack of common sense, etc. Or, lack of a sense of crisis against these behaviors." (In the Japanese new word dictionary the word is SANSEIDO)

Research on the ecology of the safety bug is becoming more and more active recently. The latest discovery in the research has now disclosed the reason there are so many safety bugs in the big enterprise. The breakthrough was made in observing that the safety bugs were highly populated in the spaces between silo organizations.

Silo organizations occur because their sense of responsibility is so big that in order to protect themselves, the different departments become trapped in a silo mentality of what is best for themselves individually instead of as a whole. Responsibility is indispensable to organizations. The bigger the organization is, the greater the responsibility. In order to satisfy these responsibilities, the big enterprises are divided into many sub-organizations. Each sub-organization's responsibility is heavy, and the individual sub-organization is expected to work hard to fulfill their responsibilities with a necessary and sufficient sense of accountability.

Imagine there are two organizations that work together to do one project. Each organization has its own responsibilities, presumably resulting in twice the responsibility. This is supposed to increase the chance of success for the project.

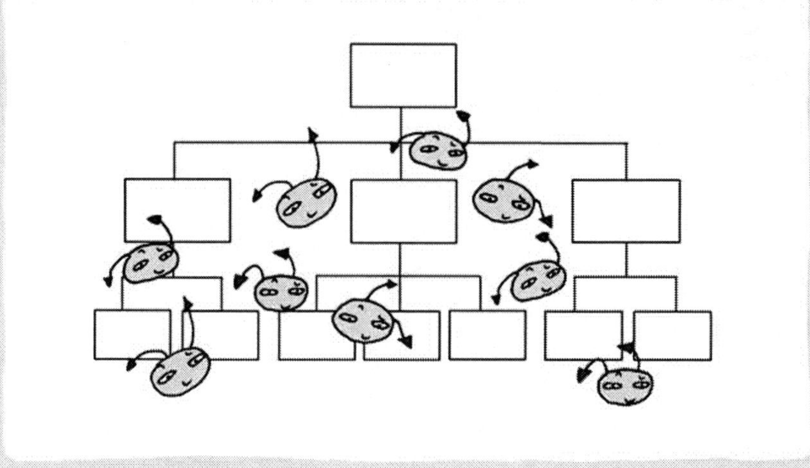

However, there is a pitfall here. A doubled sense of responsibility results in a place that provides the most comfortable atmosphere for the safety bugs to live. In other words, when one organization with a big sense of responsibility meets another organization with a big sense of responsibility, it naturally creates a place where there is excess responsibility, providing a very comfortable habitat in which safety bugs thrive.

In the day-to-day business practices of big enterprises, it is rare for one single organization to do business standing alone. Instead, the reality is that one organization needs to involve many other organizations to do daily business. The bigger the project is, the greater the number of organizations involved; this corresponds to an increase in an excess sense of responsibility. This causes a situation where there are abundant responsibilities, which are nutrients for the safety bugs, resulting in a rush of breeding behavior. Where there is abundant nutrition, safety bugs rapidly lay eggs and build massive safety bug clusters throughout the organization. This is why lots of safety bugs are observed in the spaces between the organizations, causing big enterprise disease.

This breakthrough research made it possible to develop a specific medicine to cure big enterprise disease, which is CCPM GAS. When you spray CCPM gas, safety bugs mutate into motivated bugs that practice teamwork by sharing responsibility, without excess, even in projects where many organizations are involved. Dramatic effects are being announced everywhere, but it is especially recommended to deliberately spray in the spaces between organizations.

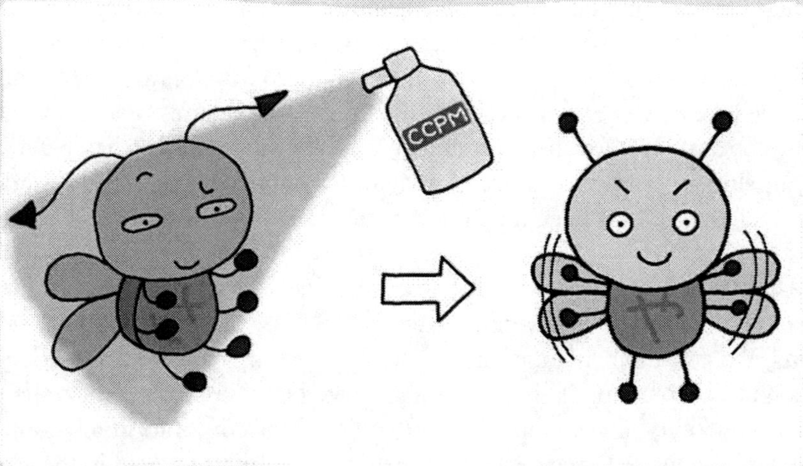

Appendix

Win-Win-Win Public Works Reform

Abstract

This paper details the findings of a case study documenting the implementation of Critical Chain Project Management (CCPM) for Government public works management in Japan. The result showed a drastic reduction of the construction duration, improved profitability at contractors, enhanced quality of work, significant improvement in motivation of all players such as Government officials and contractors, and a higher satisfaction level for local residents. It was concluded that the major contributor of this test project success is "Communication & Collaboration," while the traditional Government management, using excessive rules and manuals, causes undesirable human behaviors, reminding us that it is people who conduct tasks in projects.

1. Introduction

With the recent drastic reduction in public works activity due to the financial difficulties of the Government, the volume of orders local construction companies have received has shrunk to less than half of that in the past. Faced with this severe business environment, some local construction companies are struggling to survive, and some have already been forced into bankruptcy. At the same time, a series recent of large-scale natural disasters has raised attention to the importance of public works construction, historically mostly carried out by local construction firms. This issue is being discussed widely with increasing concern. Under these circumstances, the Government has been exploring a paradigm shift in public works management by implementing various action plans. However, there has not yet been much in the way of positive outcomes.

A one-year case study was conducted with the objective of outlining an ideal public works scenario. The study covered an analysis of the current situation and its considerations, the way implementation of a new project management methodology, and verification of the solution. This case study showed a wide-range of benefits including significant reductions in construction time, creation of corporate profit, improvement in the convenience of local residents, and furthermore, improvement in the competence levels of government officials by communication & collaboration amongst all project stakeholders.

2. Analysis of the current situation

As is often said in the industry, the problem is the gap between reality (as is) and the ideal (to be). In order to understand the project challenges, the author for Government officials from the Hokkaido Regional Development Bureau of Ministry of Land, Infrastructure and Transportation (MLIT) conducted a "Questioning Session." Over twenty managers from different divisions attended this session, where they were asked to write three responses to the question, "What is preventing you from doing a good job in public works?" The session leader then challenged, "Why? Why? Why?" to each problem given, until all the problems noted were drilled down to the root-cause issue to be solved.

3. Consideration of solutions

In the Questioning Session, three major undesirable effects were studied:

- Low contractor profits (losing money in many cases)
- Government financial difficulties
- Poor cultivation of government human resources (how to transfer experience to young people)

One of the large problems that contractors highlighted was the long downtime experienced during construction when government officials need to agree to engineering changes as a result of unexpected issues. Uncertainty is inherent in construction work. There are virtually no two construction projects that are carried out under exactly the same conditions. In particular, as nature plays an important role in most public construction, the uncertainty involved is extremely large. Thus, contractors consult government supervisors on a daily basis regarding changing construction techniques or design. These changes force delays and budget overruns, creating frustration and inconvenience among all stakeholders. Following the analysis and discussion of the findings to remedy the undesirable effects, attendees concluded that the most important and powerful solution that the government could implement was to respond to the contractors quickly. We named this effort the "One Day Response Project."[64]

To verify the direction of the solution, a "Future Reality Tree," or "FRT," was used—a tool borrowed from the "TOC Thinking Process." The FRT uses cause and effect sufficiency-logic, meaning an "If/Then" approach. This logic verifies whether a certain solution is truly effective for solving the problem.

---

64. *One Day Response* is a symbolic name which means to reply with utmost urgency. It does not mean providing all solutions in a day. It means that one should try to solve problems in a day as much as possible, but even in cases where solutions cannot be provided in a day, one should help the building constructor make plans for next steps.

Chart 1 can be read starting from the bottom: "If the One Day Response project is implemented, then public works projects finish earlier" than scheduled. Contractors will have less futile waiting time and will start making more profits even in severe situations. Furthermore, in order to reply in a day, government supervisors will act on the situation quickly, enhancing his or her management capabilities by prompting discussions with their more experienced managers. In addition, if the infrastructure is completed earlier, taxpayers/residents will be happy. If they are happy, contractors as well as government supervisors will also become happy. On top of that, economic effects from the public work will be realized earlier, and the local economy will be vitalized earlier. If collaboration between government supervisors and contractors is enhanced, the quality of the public work will improve. If the quality of public works improves, in accordance with the new government law "Quality of Public Works," contractors can be chosen, not only by cost, but also by quality history and technology proposals. If good-quality infrastructure is provided earlier than scheduled, demonstrating economic effects earlier as well as enabling contractors to make profits, tax income will increase. Thus, public works will contribute to financial reconstruction while providing good-quality infrastructure. In other words, adoption of the One Day Response Project was confirmed to be an extremely powerful remedy for the three problems mentioned before. Looking once again at this chart, we recognized the **"One Day Response Project was confirmed to be a project that enables public works to return to its origin."**

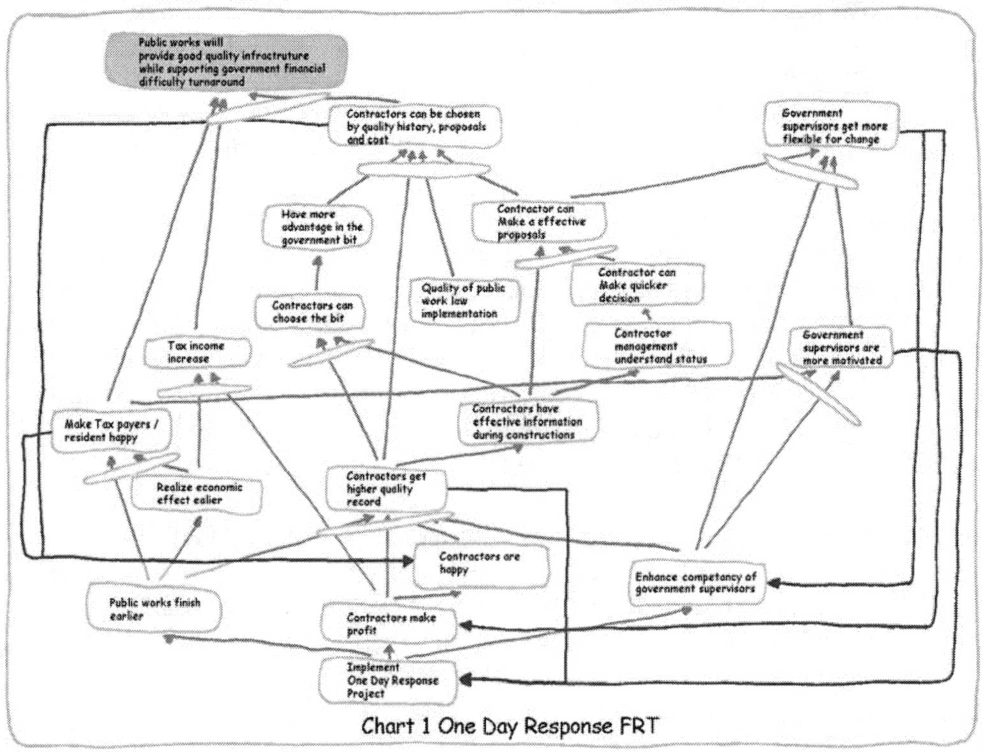

Chart 1 One Day Response FRT

4. One Day Response Project Evaluation

In the Sapporo road office, Hokkaido Regional Department Bureau of MLIT, a young government supervisor was instructed to avoid downtime in construction by providing One Day Response to contractors. He managed five sites simultaneously. After completion of all sites, a letter was brought to our attention. Here is a part of the letter with the permission of the sender, Shinji Hirogami, foreman of Sunagogumi Corporation.

Lastly, we were able to make a higher profit than in the original plan. I feel that the approach of the government supervisor was different from projects in the past; he acted in a way so as to allow construction to proceed smoothly. Or rather, I should say that it made me feel as though he himself was carrying out the project together with us as a team. It became a wonderful construction project where quick response and good communication enabled good quality work to be completed much earlier than original plan, which pleased the local residents. Everyone who worked on the site felt a sense of satisfaction. I would like to express my heart-felt appreciation.
November 25, 2005
Shinji Hirogami, Sunagogumi Corporation

In order to find out why such a result as mentioned in this letter was made possible, the author visited the government supervisor who received this letter. His comments were:

- Forecasting and simulating are important in construction work in order to avoid downtime.

- It was easy to handle the work because Sunagogumi, the contractor in charge, had a strong awareness for their work, and their unique progress reports allowed us to visualize the situation. Initially, I felt rather concerned because the duration for each task was estimated very aggressively without any "SABA" (a Japanese word for safety in each task). However, I found that as they controlled the schedule by using buffer aggregated at the end, it was in fact intuitively easy to understand[65].

- If the contractors present a schedule without any SABA, a sense of trust is born, making people feel that they are working together on the construction. It is easier to work in this case compared to cases in which contractors provide ordinary schedules full of hidden safety in each task.

His boss, the group manager said, "The most crucial problem in construction is the downtime which delays the completion of public works projects and sometimes causes budget overruns. Uncertainty always exists in public works projects. Thus, quick deci-

65. It was after the construction work was finished that the foreman in charge found out that he had in fact empirically been using a process very similar to "Critical Chain Project Management" (CCPM) methodology, a solution for managing projects also based in the Theory of Constraints.

sions and responses are important so that work progresses. Therefore, I gather members in my section on a daily basis to ensure the work has not stopped. If there are any problems, we deal with it quickly as a team. There are some cases in which we are unable to immediately reply, and the work must be stopped. In such cases, we check with the contractor as to how long they can wait, and make every effort to reply by their deadline." His words precisely indicate that his team is practicing One Day Response for not stopping the work. On the other hand, they also said that whether they can respond quickly also depends on the ability of the contractors. No matter how committed the government supervisor may be in responding quickly, he or she sometimes cannot do so depending on the proposal and the communication skills of the contractors. In the case of the construction work Sunagogumi handled, the supervisor found he could do his job far more easily.

Sunagogumi has adopted Critical Chain Project Management (CCPM) to shorten construction time. What is especially unique in this method is the aggressive task duration estimates (which eliminate SABA in each task and assign a 50% probability of success) and the placement of a project buffer, aggregated and added to the end of the project, which can be used to protect the due date from variations in the project. This buffer is then managed by monitoring the consumption percentage of the buffer. This can be said to be **verbalizing the "DANDORI HACHIBU" (Preparation is 80% of the project success), which had been practiced as tacit knowledge for many years in the Japanese construction industry among excellent foremen.**

The government supervisor felt that the method used by Sunagogumi of communicating honestly without SABA made it easier for him to understand what was happening. It enabled him to forecast and study any necessary changes in construction, in a working relationship based on trust between the two parties. As a result, less effort and time were required compared with the other four contractors.

5. Collaboration through Sharing the Buffer

In CCPM, the consumption level of the buffer is shown in green, yellow and red in order of ascending seriousness. By monitoring the consumption level of the buffer and the changes in the color of the buffer, it is possible to take necessary preventive actions far before project delays actually occur, and even to avoid them happening. In other words, by looking at the indicator that shows the consumption level of the buffer, and by monitoring which tasks are consuming the buffer, one can take necessary measures before it becomes too late. If contractors use this method and share the status of buffer consumption with the government supervisor, any delay in response by the government supervisor becomes clear—it consumes buffer and the buffer color is changed for the worse. Thus, it can be seen that a shift will occur in the awareness of the government supervisor to make decisions and respond to the contractors more quickly. Convention-

ally, contractors have the tendency to hide SABA as much as possible as safety to prepare for uncertainty and to meet the due date. This tendency can be observed not only in the construction industry, but also in general industry. **It is a valuable lesson to learn that by showing the schedule without safety and by sharing the buffer, cooperation/teamwork is much enhanced.** This can be attributed to the fact that by revealing the true picture, communication between the two parties was accelerated. Most people who implemented CCPM have the impression that communication is greatly enhanced thanks to buffer management. They regard CCPM as a communication vehicle. In this case, it seems the simple and easy buffer mechanism enhances communication and creates teamwork throughout construction sites.

6. Human Resource Development

Both the government supervisor and contractor foreman made comments that human resource growth was cultivated during this project due to communication and teamwork enhancement—where they mutually learned from each other. Some even said that cultivation of human resources was above all the largest result from this case. The findings of the author from the interviewing the government supervisor and his manager and are:

- The young supervisor started taking the initiative to consult with the managers without hesitation, making the job as manager much easier.
- By consulting sooner, issues were finalized sooner. As a result, over-time work was reduced, allowing people to go home early.
- The young supervisor felt that he really managed this project with the contractor through teamwork.
- The young supervisor felt more motivated because local residents appreciated their work.

In order to educate young people, they must learn by experience. It seems that the One Day Response Project accelerates learning speed and provides an excellent environment for young people to learn things by experience.

7. "Communication, Collaboration and Commitment" Management

What was interesting in this case was that most of the people involved mentioned that they found their work more interesting and rewarding. In order to implement One Day Response, the supervisor in charge needs to closely communicate with contractors. Furthermore, he needs to do everything necessary to advance the work, always consulting with his superior. Finally, according to the level of consumption of the buffer, it becomes very clear what actions to take in advance to avoid any delay in work on the project.

In short, the communication among all the concerned parties regarding the project was greatly accelerated using One Day Response Project. When one considers this, it suggests that there is a paradigm shift in the management method. Chart 2 is a positioning map showing this paradigm shift. By plotting from easy to complex on the vertical axis and from communication to control on the horizontal bar, we can obtain interesting findings. The quadrant at the bottom left shows management by Command & Control, used in a traditional pyramid-shaped organizational structure. Here, the logic that "The Headquarters must control the site," and "The government must control the contractors," plays a very important role. The job description must be clearly defined and people become preoccupied with making manuals and rules in order to control people, as if they were soldiers. Unfortunately, this method leads to "making people work according to the manual, losing creativity of working on their own." Thus, people end up carrying out their work with the feeling of "being forced to work." It is only natural that in such an environment, achievements are obtained with difficulty. Furthermore, with this method, since documentation must exist assuming all types of problems and issues, massive manuals and rules are made as a result. It is almost impossible for people to read, understand and act upon mountains of instructions correctly. People quickly learn that in the midst of incomprehensible and massive manuals and rules, it is safer and more advantageous to "spend time without making serious blunders." They understand that heavy penalties await them if they disobey what is written in the manuals and rules. It is difficult to carry on work when one is bound hand and foot by complex manuals and rules. If a person in such a situation is asked to submit a progress report, he or she will report in a way that follows the format but is superficial in content, in order to technically meet the reporting requirements while dealing with all the troublesome work he or she is bogged down with. Then if there are problems, it leads to much tighter control. The Command & Control culture gets more solid, while people lose flexibility in doing their job.

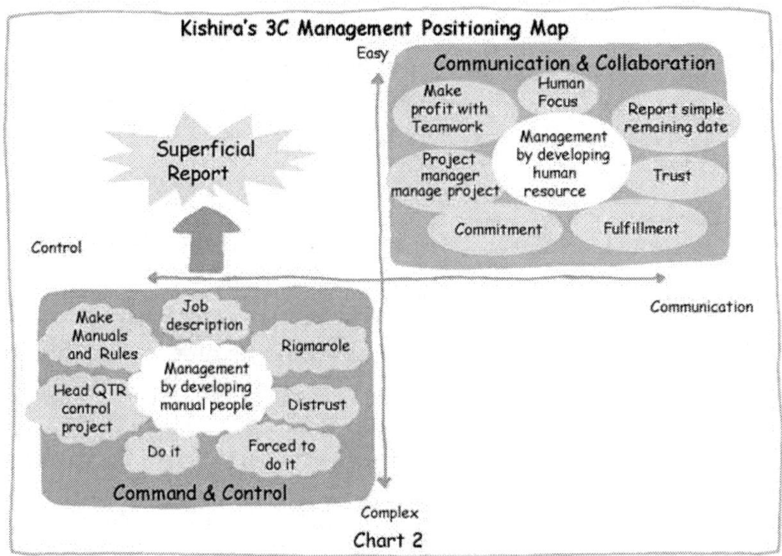

Chart 2

On the other hand, the quadrant at the top right shows "Communication & Collaboration". **People carry out Projects.** Projects contain uncertainty due to their very nature. The importance of communication through dialogue among the team is immeasurable. Considering this, it can be said that **projects will produce higher output only through people sharing their wisdom and conducting discussions in front of the whiteboard.** The project leader manages the site and reports achievements to headquarters, carrying out the project as a team. **Through Communicating & Collaboration with others, people share "a sense of challenge" and "fulfillment," and will make the commitment of their own will to work on the project.**

In the quadrant at the bottom left, Command & Control, management leads by making people work according to the manual ("manual people"), while in the quadrant at the top right, Communication & Collaboration, management can be called "management to 'cultivate people.'" If one understands the reality that projects are carried out by people, priority should be placed on how to motivate people. Considering this, it is natural that management of "cultivating people" will produce much more output. The people involved in this case study consider the greatest factor for success was the existence of Communication & Collaboration, creating Commitment to do a good job among all project members.

8. Future plan

This case suggests the One Day Response Project on the government side will create a substantial synergetic effect by combining it with CCPM on the contractor side. In order to turn these findings into statistically meaningful analyses, there is a need to verify them widely, using public works projects of different size and types. MLIT announced the acceptance of One Day Response as formal policy in March 2007, and now hundreds of construction sites throughout Japan are evaluating the effects.

On May 8, 2007, a "Win-Win-Win Public Works Management Transformation Forum" was held in Tokyo. More than 500 people attended, including high-level MLIT and other government officials, as well as construction companies from across Japan. It announced the "Declaration of Win-Win-Win Public Works Management Transformation" as follows:

"We strongly remind ourselves of our very important responsibility in public works to secure people's safety and national land safety. To realize the maximum benefit for society, both government officials and contractors must work together by providing better products with increased speed. This brings benefits to all residents, to government and to contractors and contributes to overcoming the financial difficulties of the Japanese government. We declare herewith we strongly advocate Win-Win-Win Public Works Reform."

9. Conclusion

Key success factors of this case study are underlined in its evaluation—sharing essential problems in planning, and managing human psychological factors in execution. Again, needless to say, CCPM methodology provided excellent guidance to all project members. In brief, human-centric project management is the core benefit proven in this case study.

I would like to thank Mr. Hijiri Okudaira, Director-General of Ministry of Land, Information and Transportation (MLIT) and Mr. Keigo Yanagiya, general manager of the Wakkanai office Hokkaido regional development bureau MLIT for giving me many valuable comments and direction. I received suggestions and guidance from Mr. Kazuo Yamane, Executive Director of Research Institute of Construction. I also appreciate the stimulating discussion and guidance from Mr. Shinji Yamaguchi, director of Yuzawa office MLIT.

Powerful Magic Words Summary

It has been said that a powerful solution starts with powerful questions. The following are a few simple yet powerful questions that we have been successfully applying and refining across several locations in Japan. We hope you find them equally revealing.

Step 1 : Plan

SURIAWASE discussion

"What are the objectives?"
"Is there anything else?"
"Does the ODSC incorporate all key stakeholders' perspectives (financial, customer, operation process, employee, corporate philosophy, corporate social responsibility)?"
"What are the deliverables?"
"Is there anything else?"
"What are the success criteria?"
"Is there anything else?"
"Will achieving this ODSC make you proud of your accomplishment?"
"What else would the project need to accomplish to make you proud?"

DANDORI HACHIBU discussion

"What tasks must be completed immediately before this task can be started?"
"Are there any other tasks that must fi rst be completed?"
"If you do A, then you can do B, correct?'YUTORI creation discussion

YUTORI creation discussion

"Goju Goju Desuka?"(Is it fifty-fifty?)
"Is there any good way to reduce this task estimate and still have a fair chance of meeting the estimate?"
"What can management do for you that would help you reduce this task estimate?"

Step 2 : Execution

SENTE KANRI discussion

"How many working days remain until you are done with this task?"
"What problems, if any do you anticipate in completing this task?"
"What you are waiting for?"
"How can we help you?"
"Can you offer a help, especially from the project in green?"

Step 3 : Review

KAIZEN discussion

"What were you waiting for?"
"Why was the task delayed?"
"What did you learn from this experience?"
"What steps will you take to ensure that it does not happen again?"

A Process Of OnGoing Improvement

References

Goldratt, E.M. *Critical Chain*. Great Barrington, MA: The North River Press, 1997

Goldratt, E.M. *The Goal*. 2nd revised edition. Great Barrington: The North River Press, 1992

Kanai, T., "Motivation Theory for all Working People." NTT Publishing, 2006 (In Japanese)

Kishira, Y., *Project Management to Exceed your Goal*. Tokyo: Chukei Publishing, 2005 (In Japanese)

Kishira, Y., *Transformation Management*. Tokyo: Chukei Publishing, 2006 (In Japanese)

Kishira, Y., *Win-Win-Win Public Work Management Transformation.* Tokyo: Chukei Publishing, 2007 (In Japanese)

Ohara, S., "Project & Program Management for Enterprise Innovation." H&I, 2002 (In Japanese)

Ohno, Taiichi. *Toyota Production System* New York: Productivity Press, 1988

Oxford Advanced Learner's Dictionary. 6th Revised ed. London: Oxford University Press, 2002